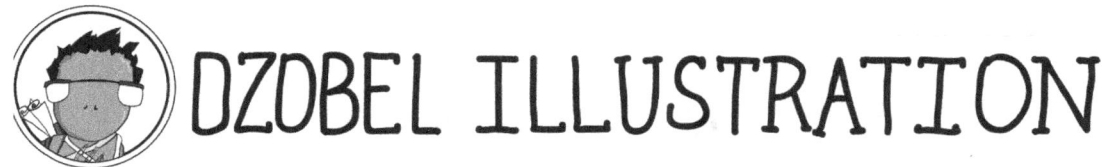

Cover and all images by:
David Zobel
dzobel illustration

2017 by

© dzobel illustration

Baltimore, MD

david@dzobel.com

All rights reserved. No part of this publication may be reproduced, stored in a retrieval system, or transmitted, in any form or by any means, electronic, mechanical, photocopying, recording and/or otherwise, without the prior written permission from dzobel illustration.

Printed and bound in the
United States of America

First Printing 2017

All images are drawn in Sketchbook Pro. All images are created and drawn by David Zobel.

| David Zobel | dzobel.com | 443.691.3914 |
| Designer/Illustrator | david@dzobel.com | |

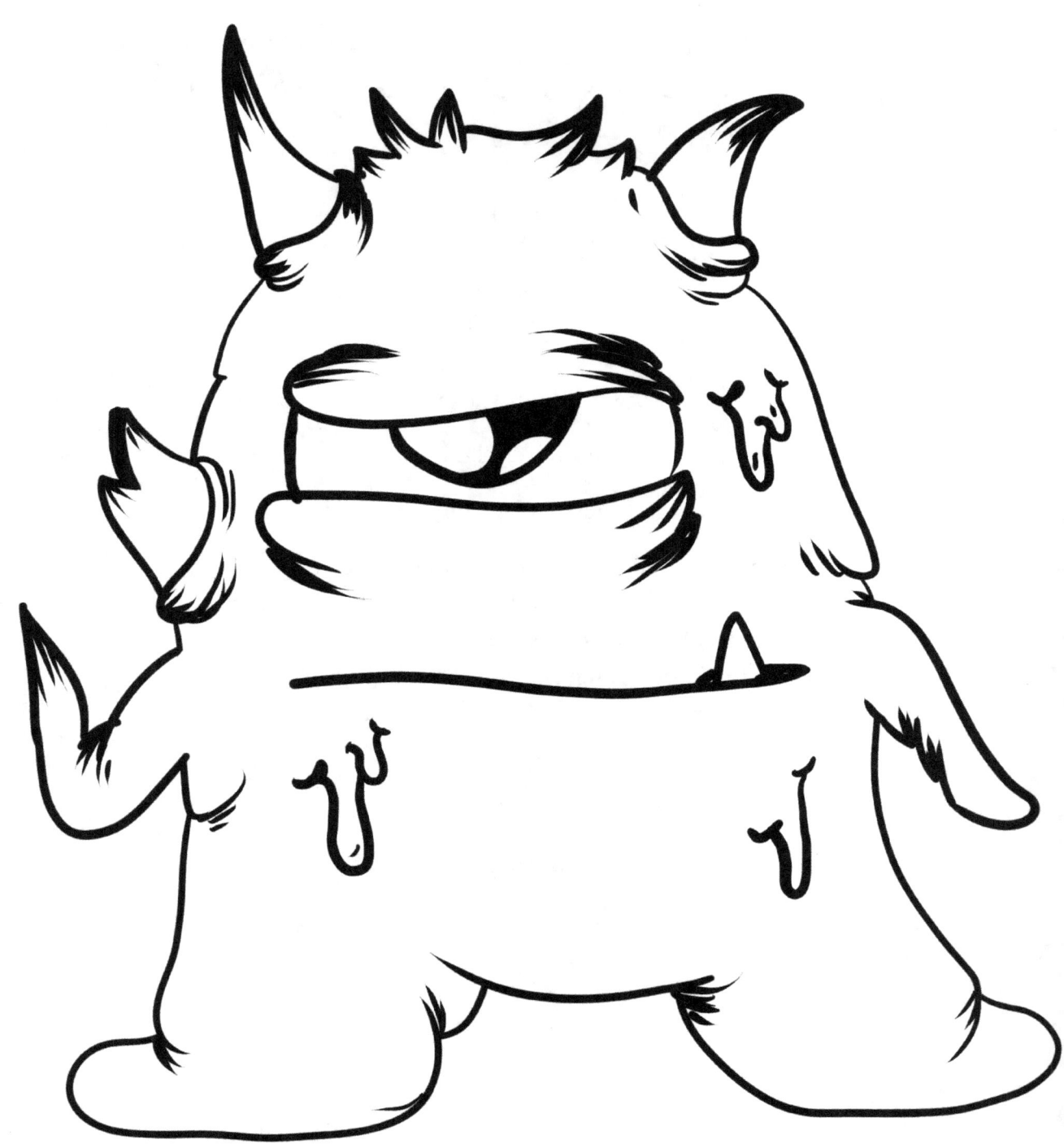

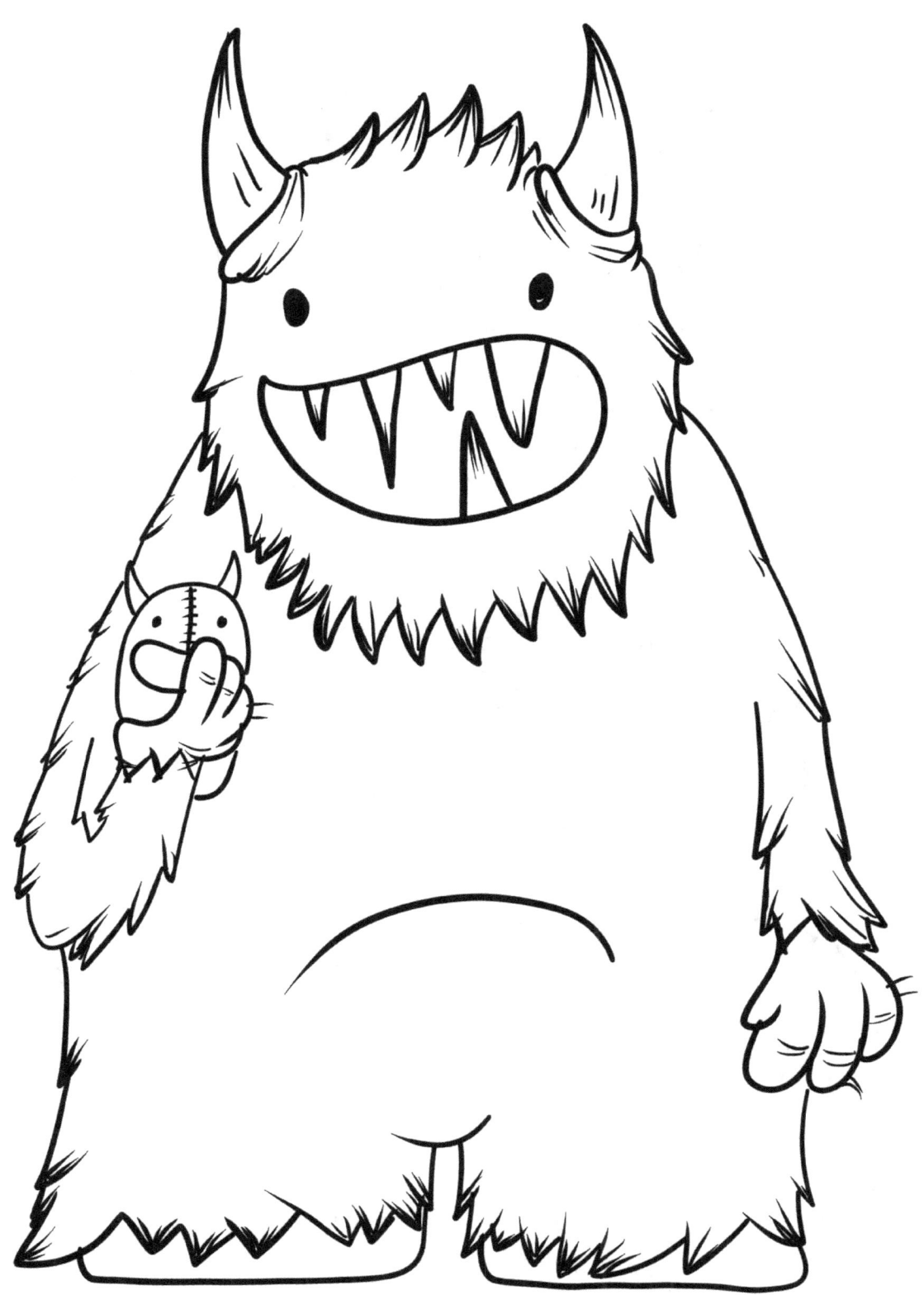

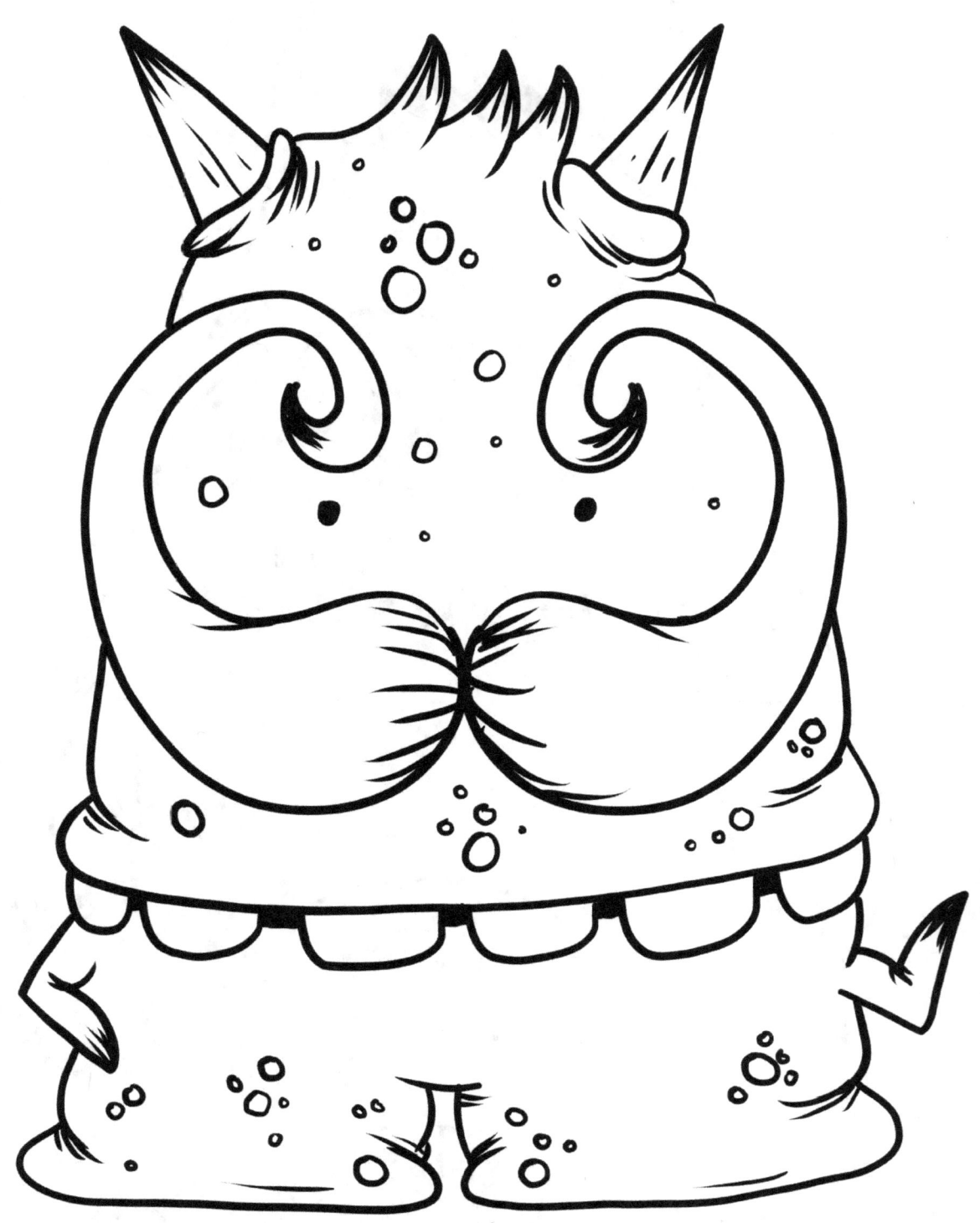

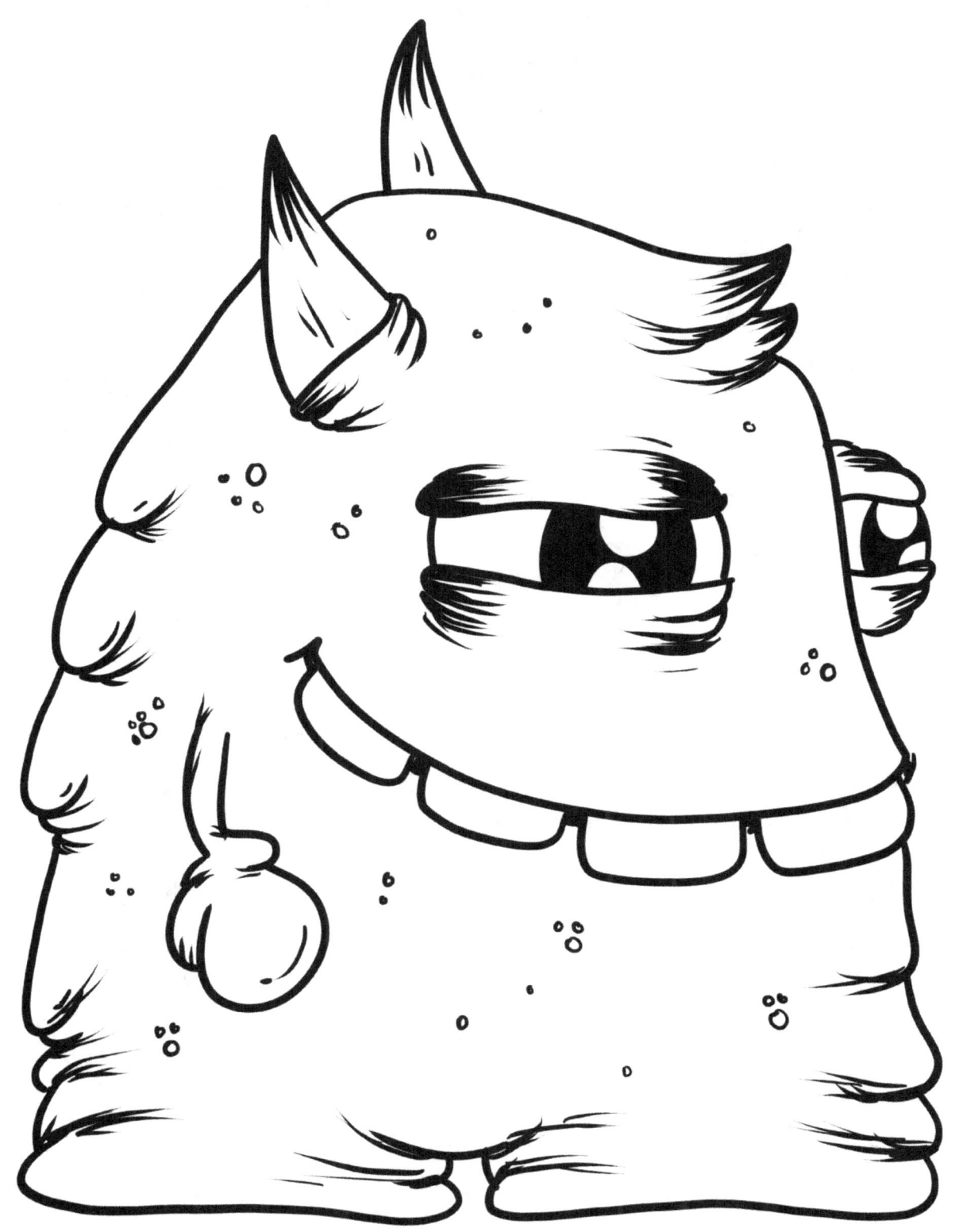

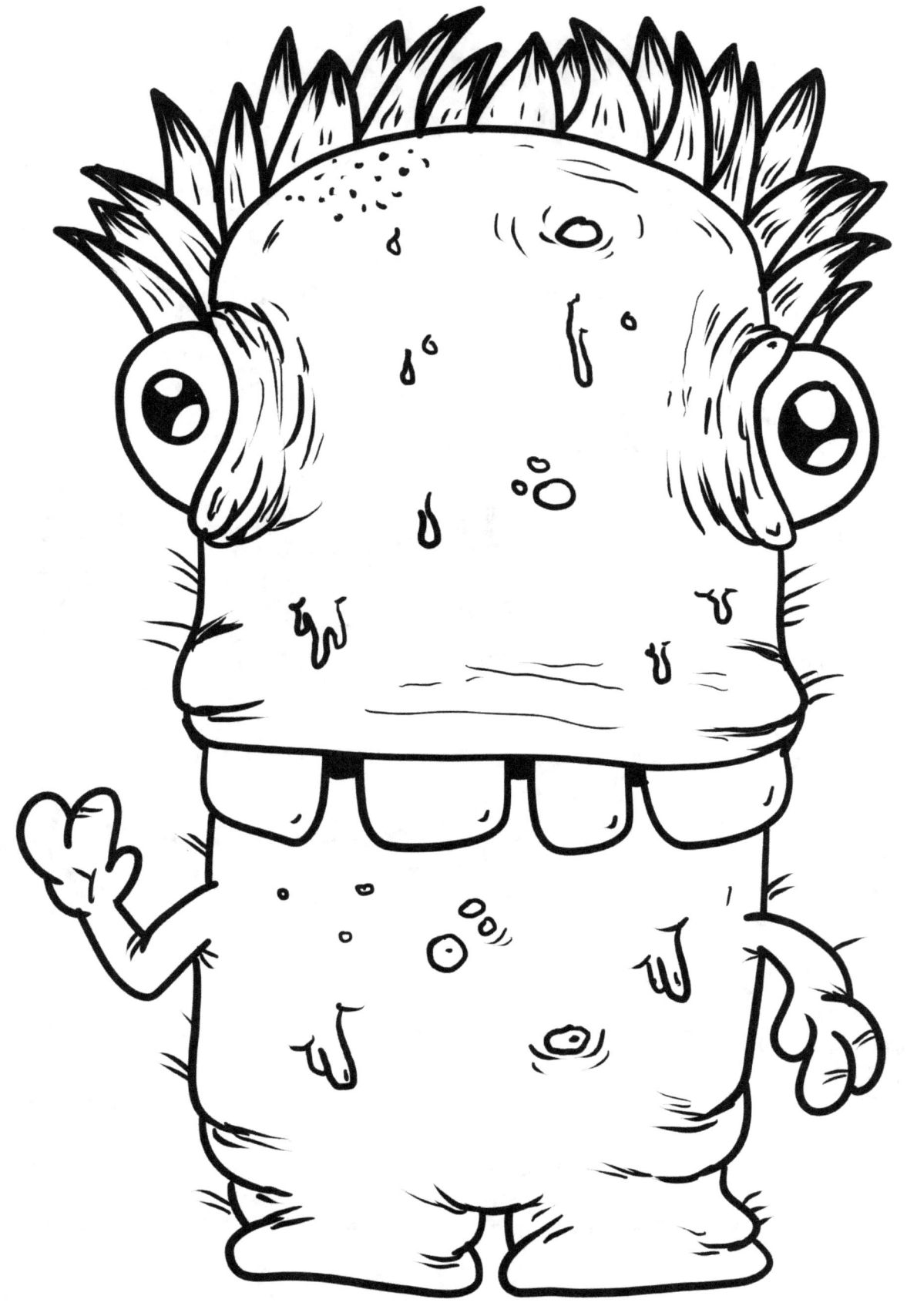

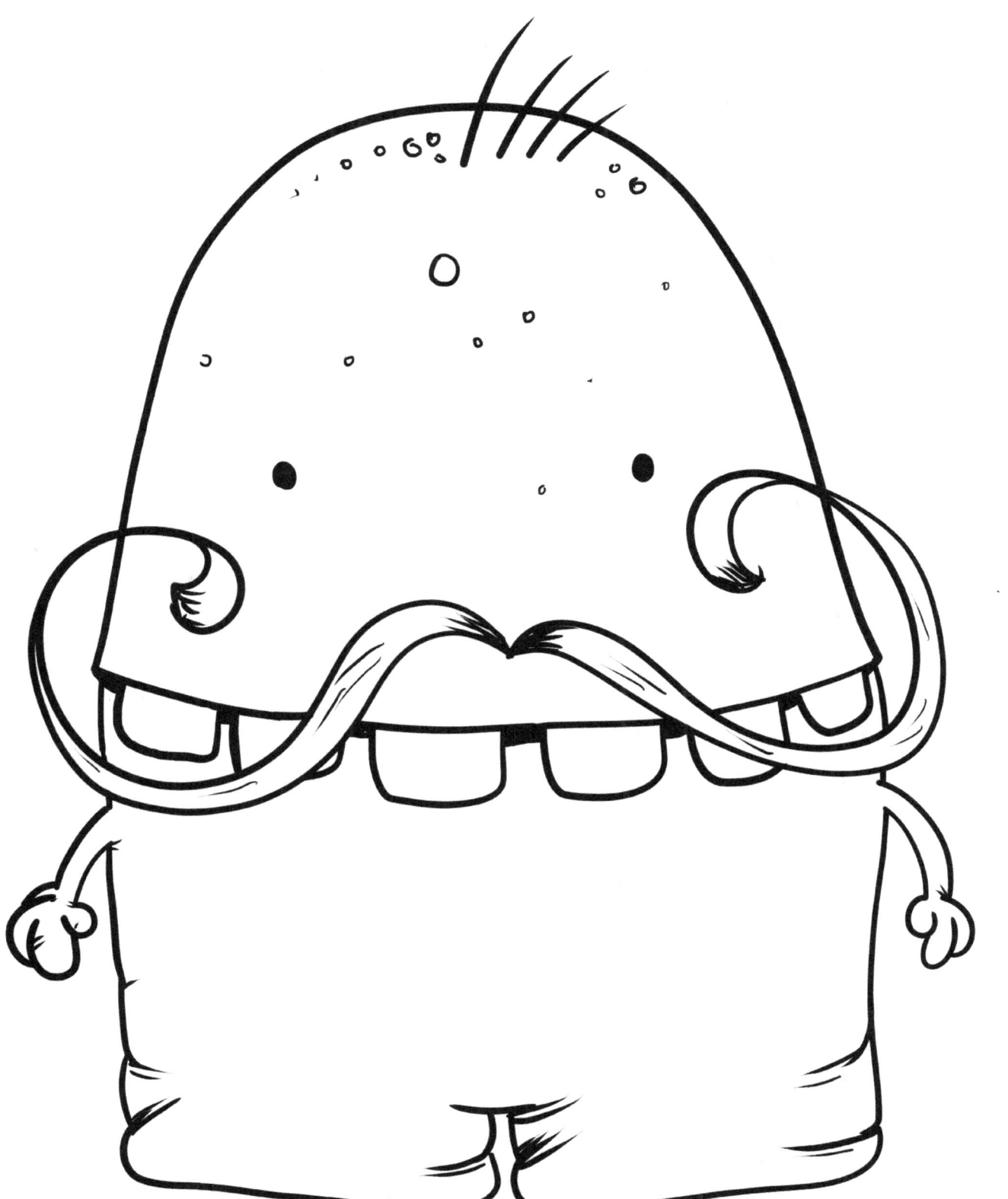

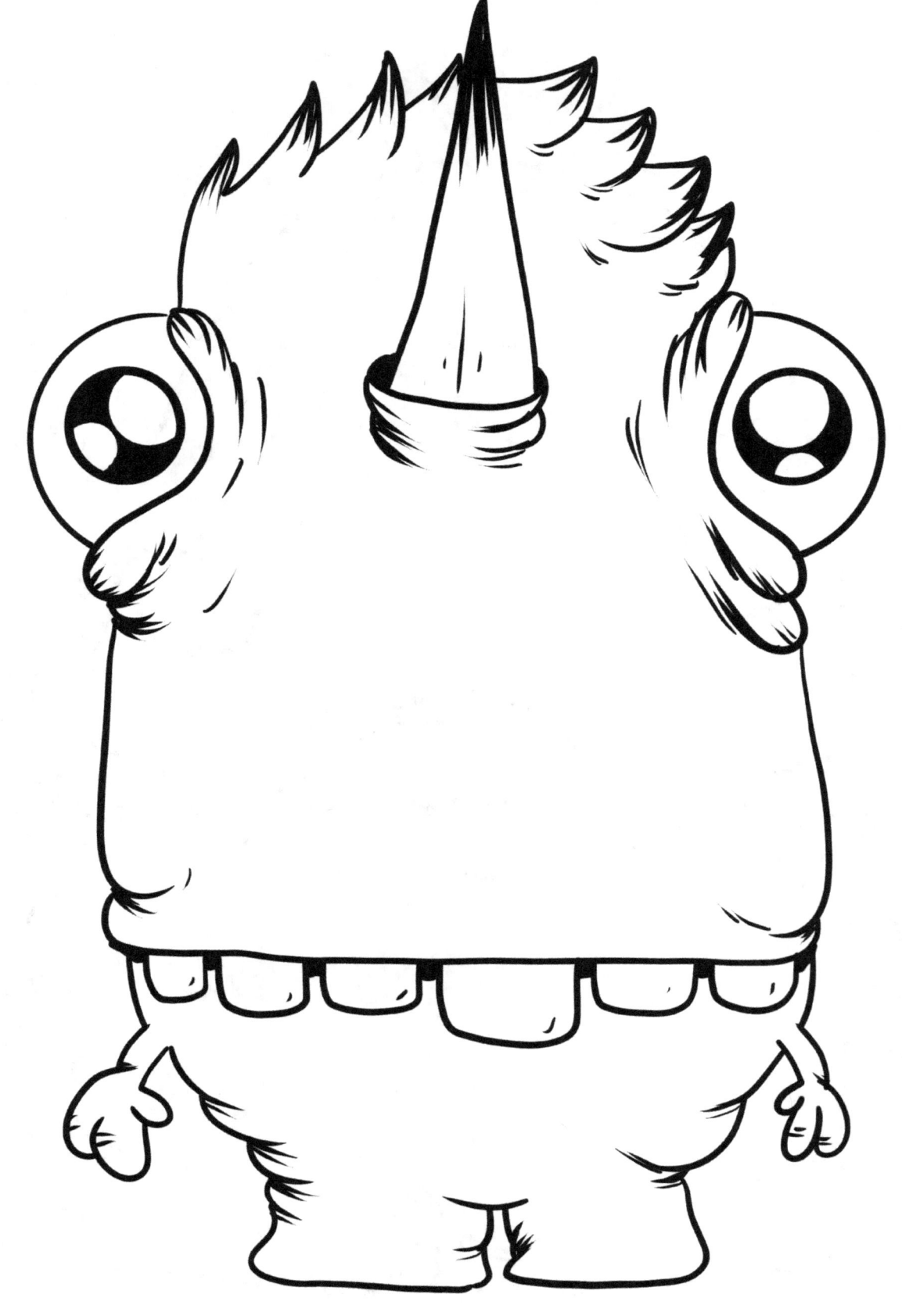

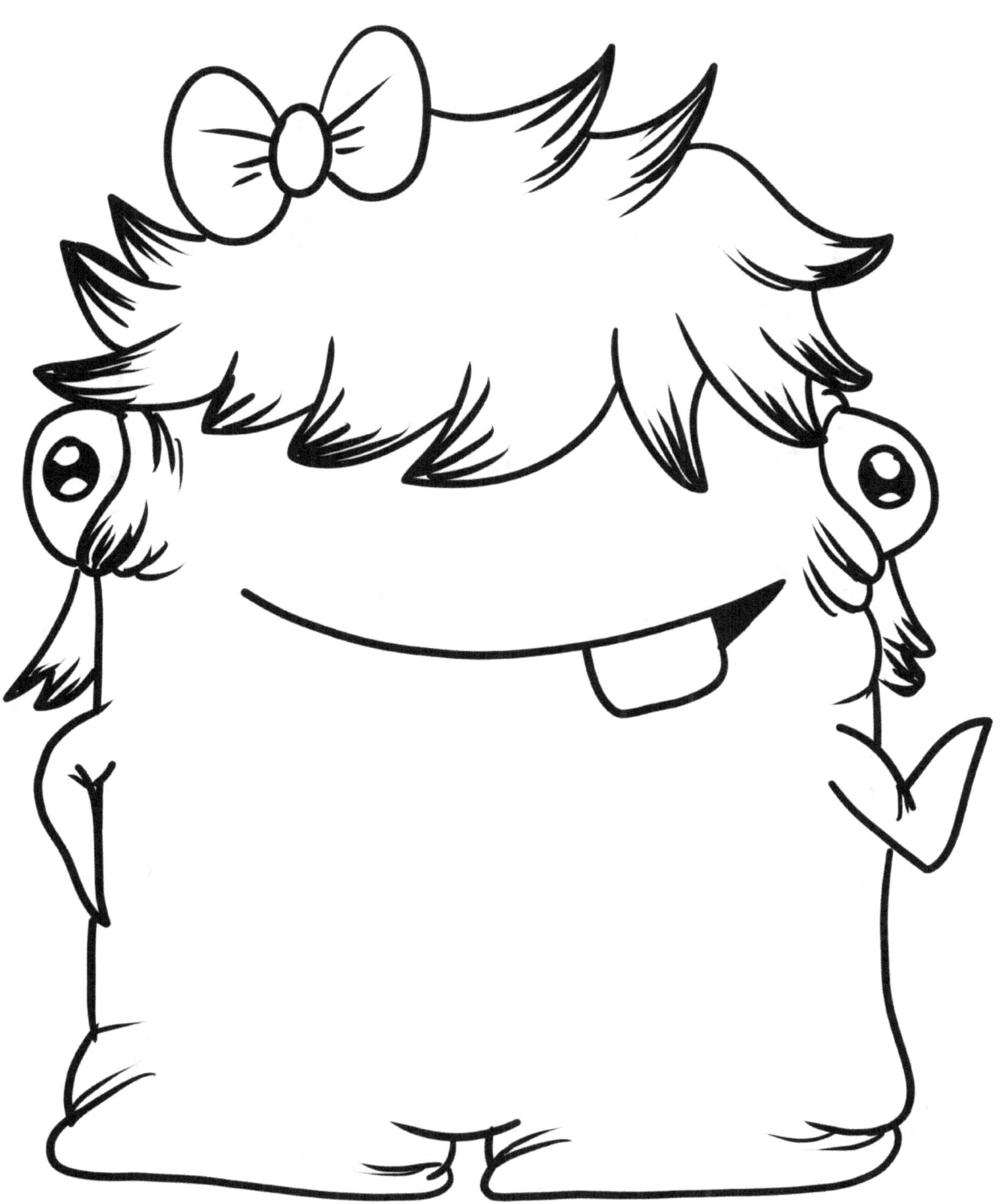

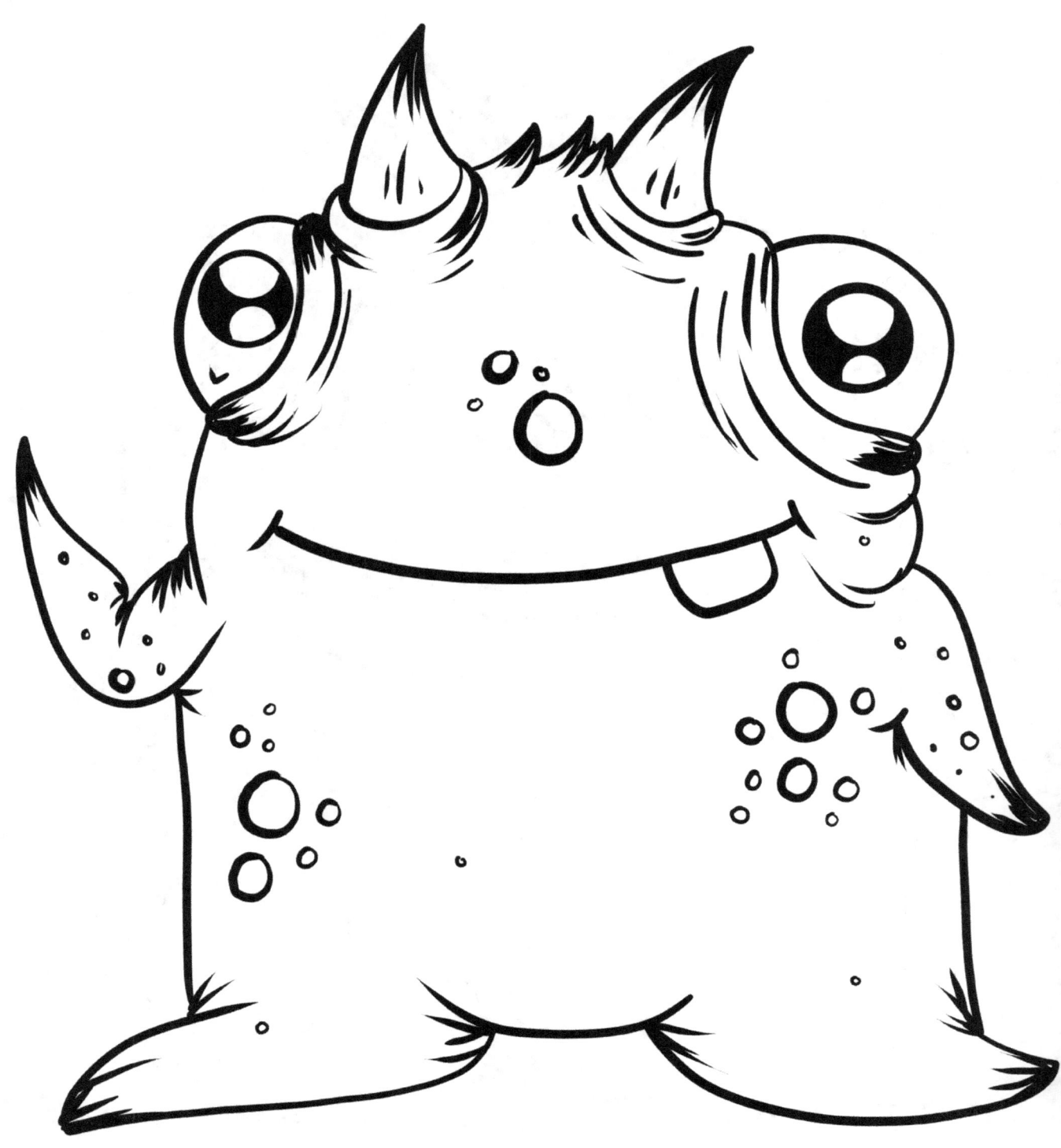

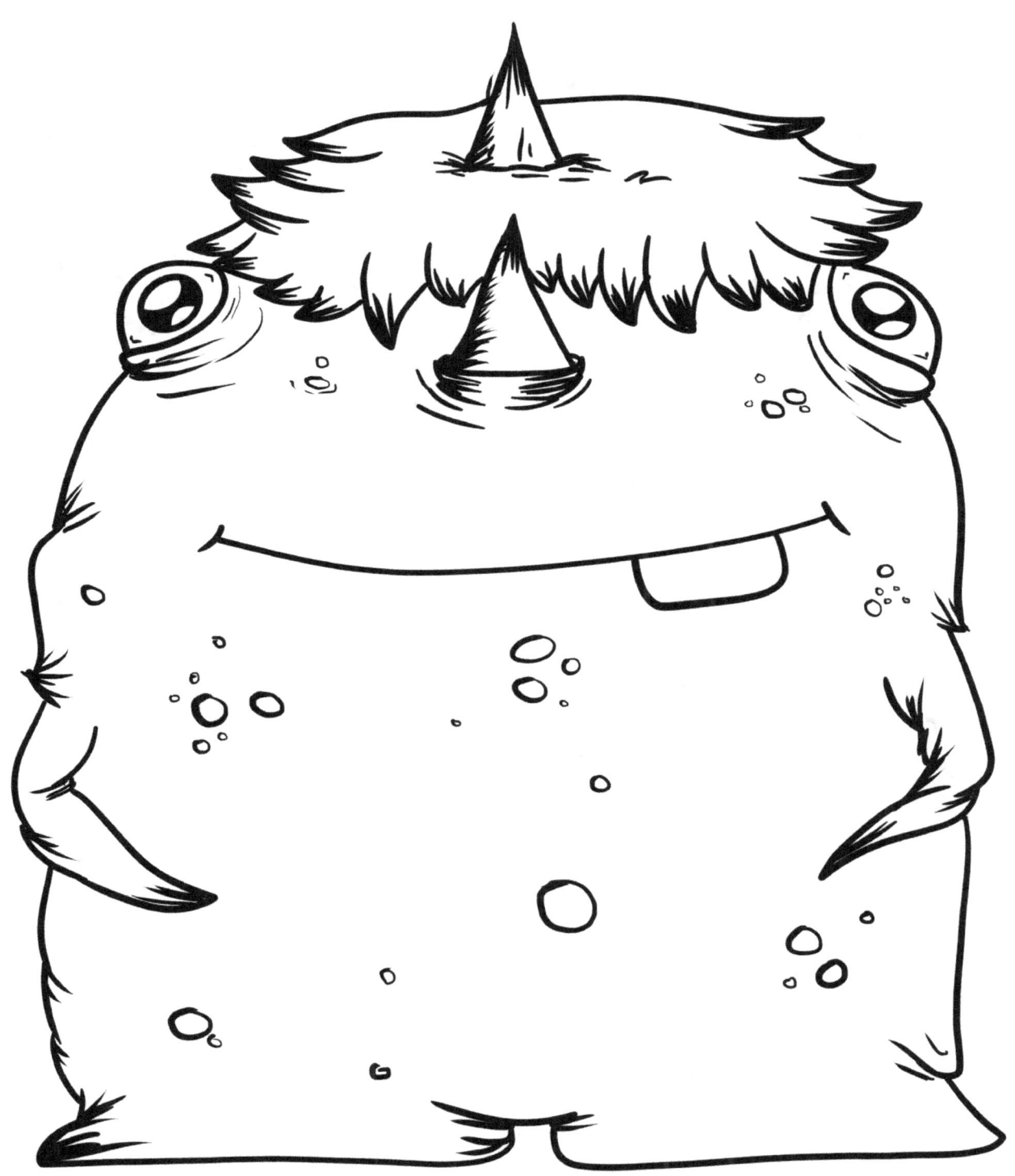

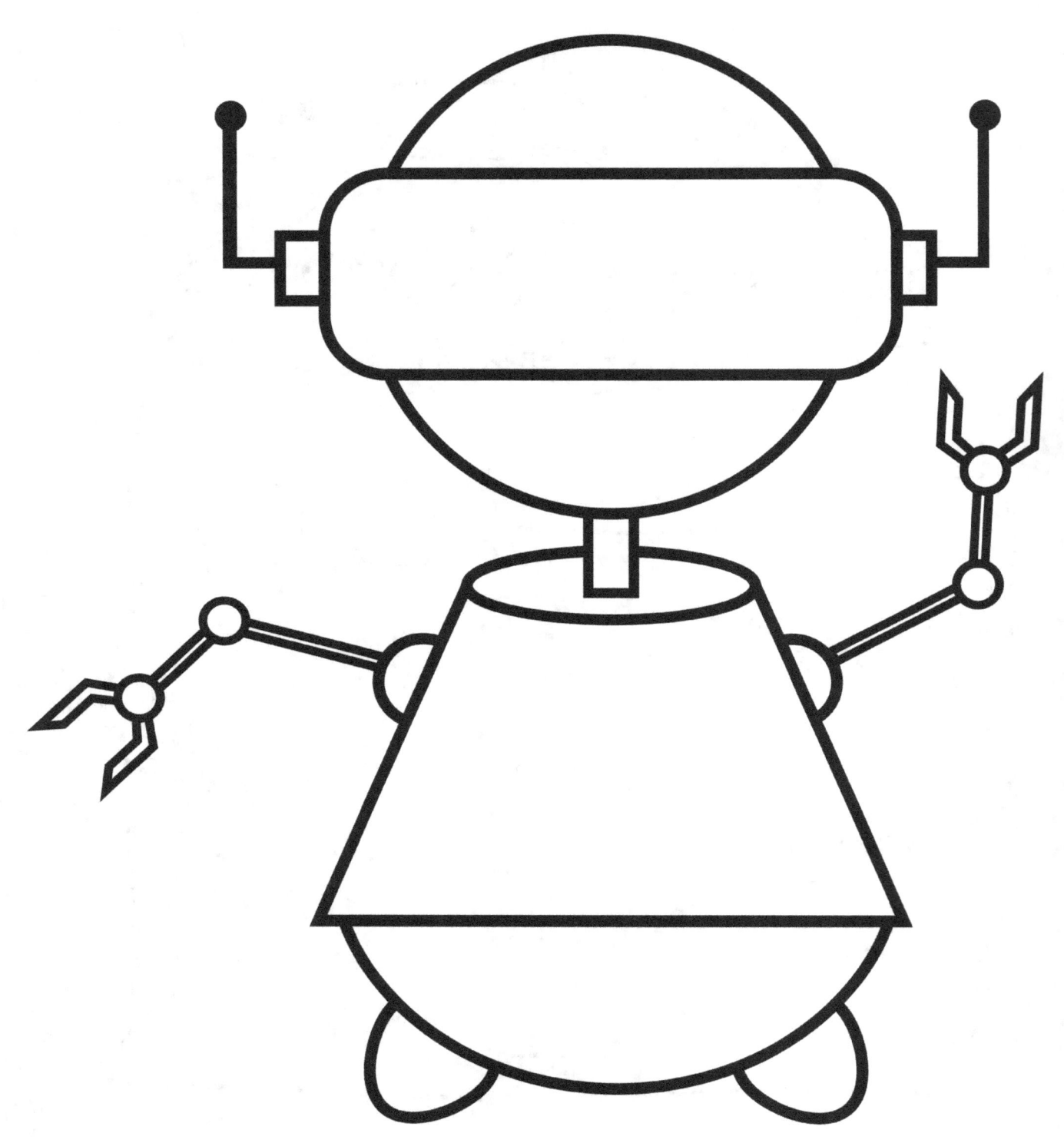

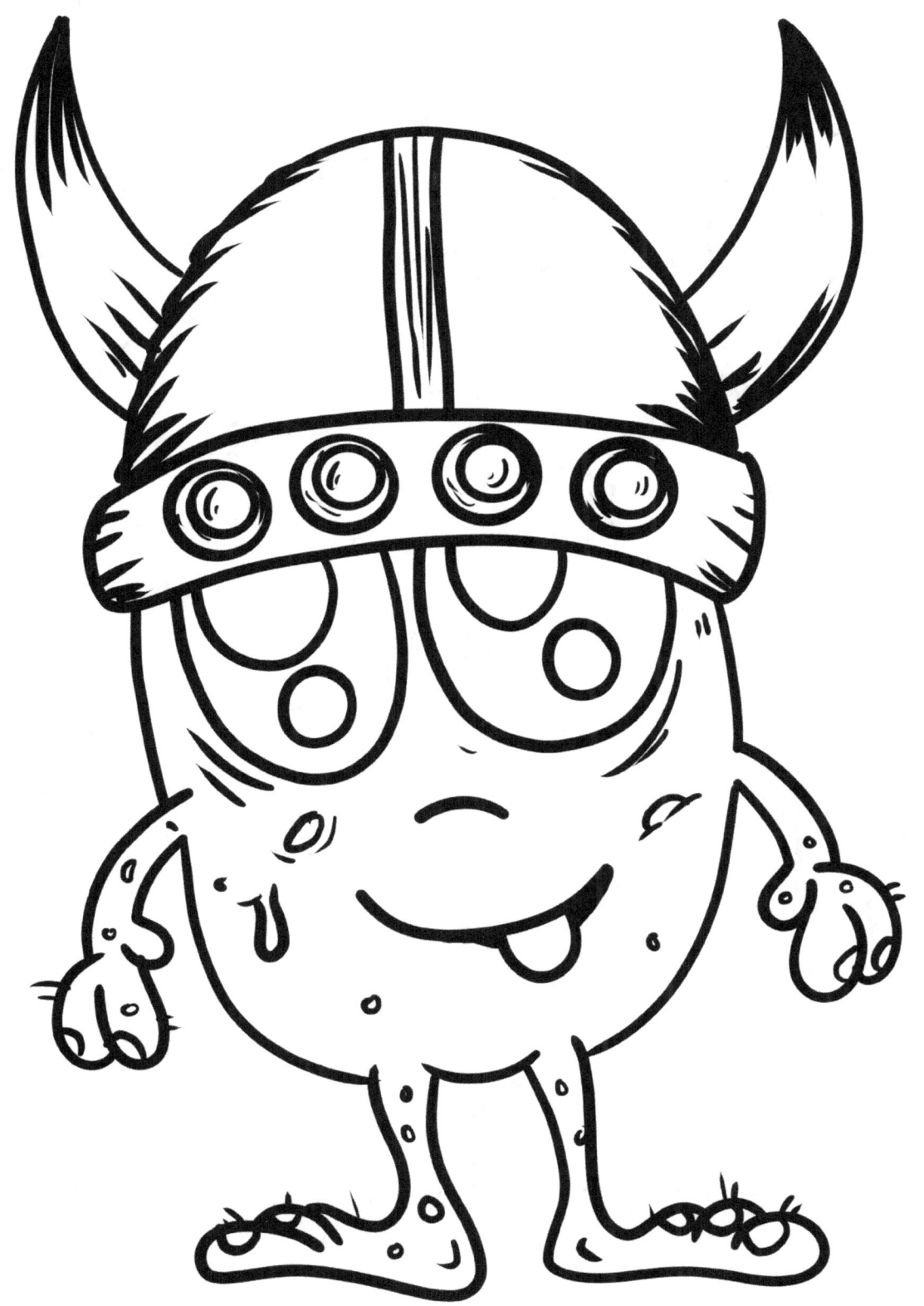

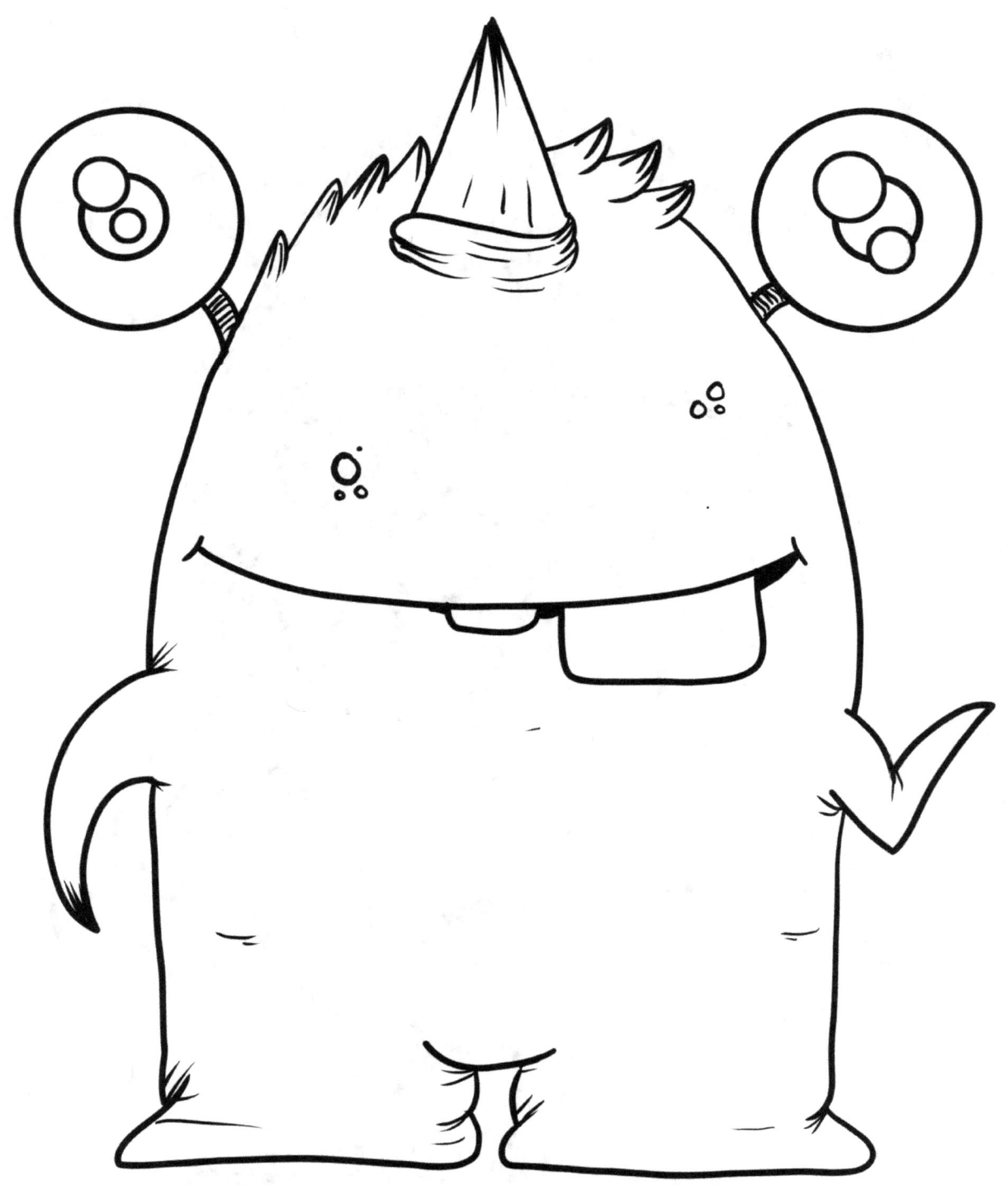

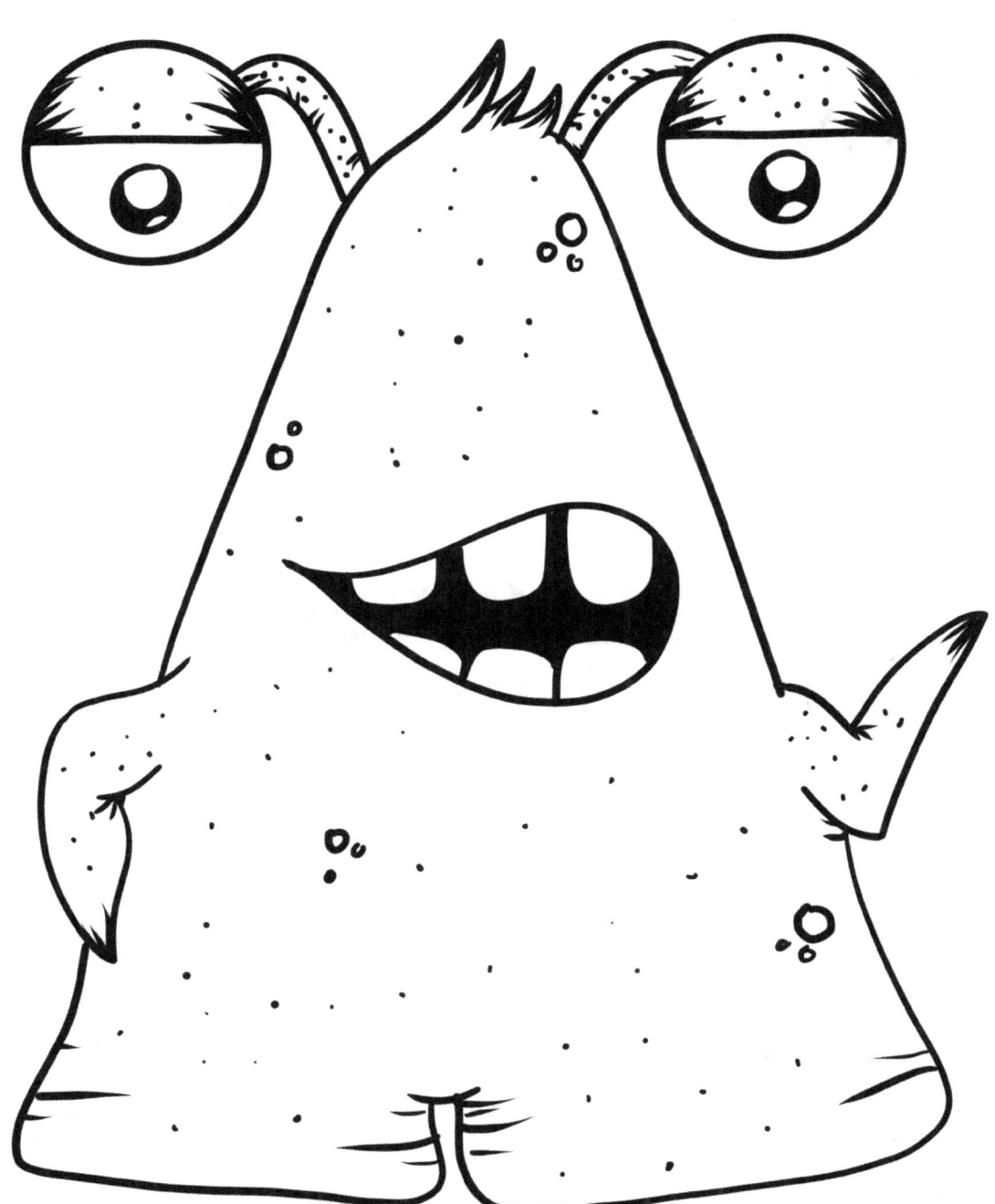

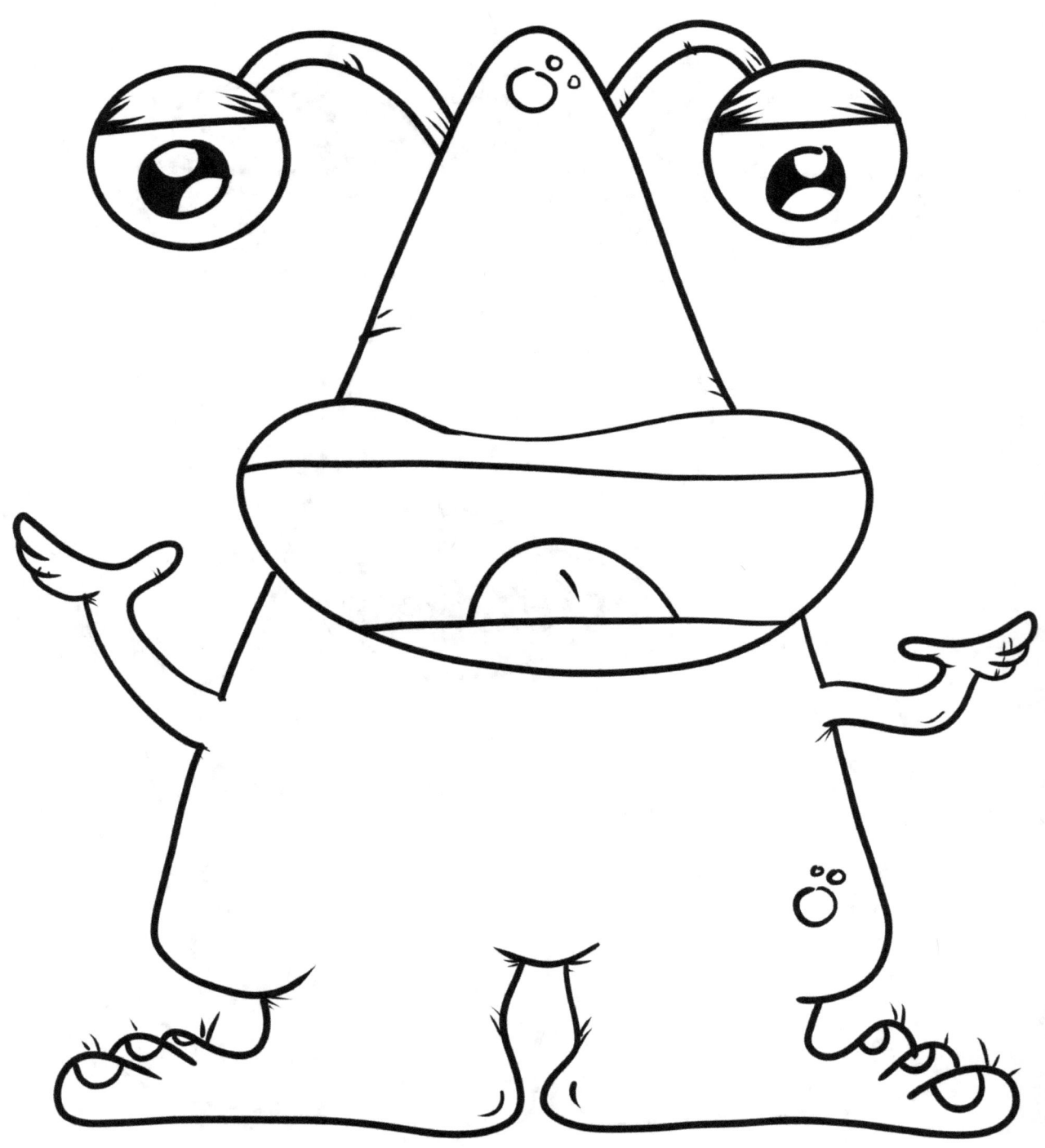

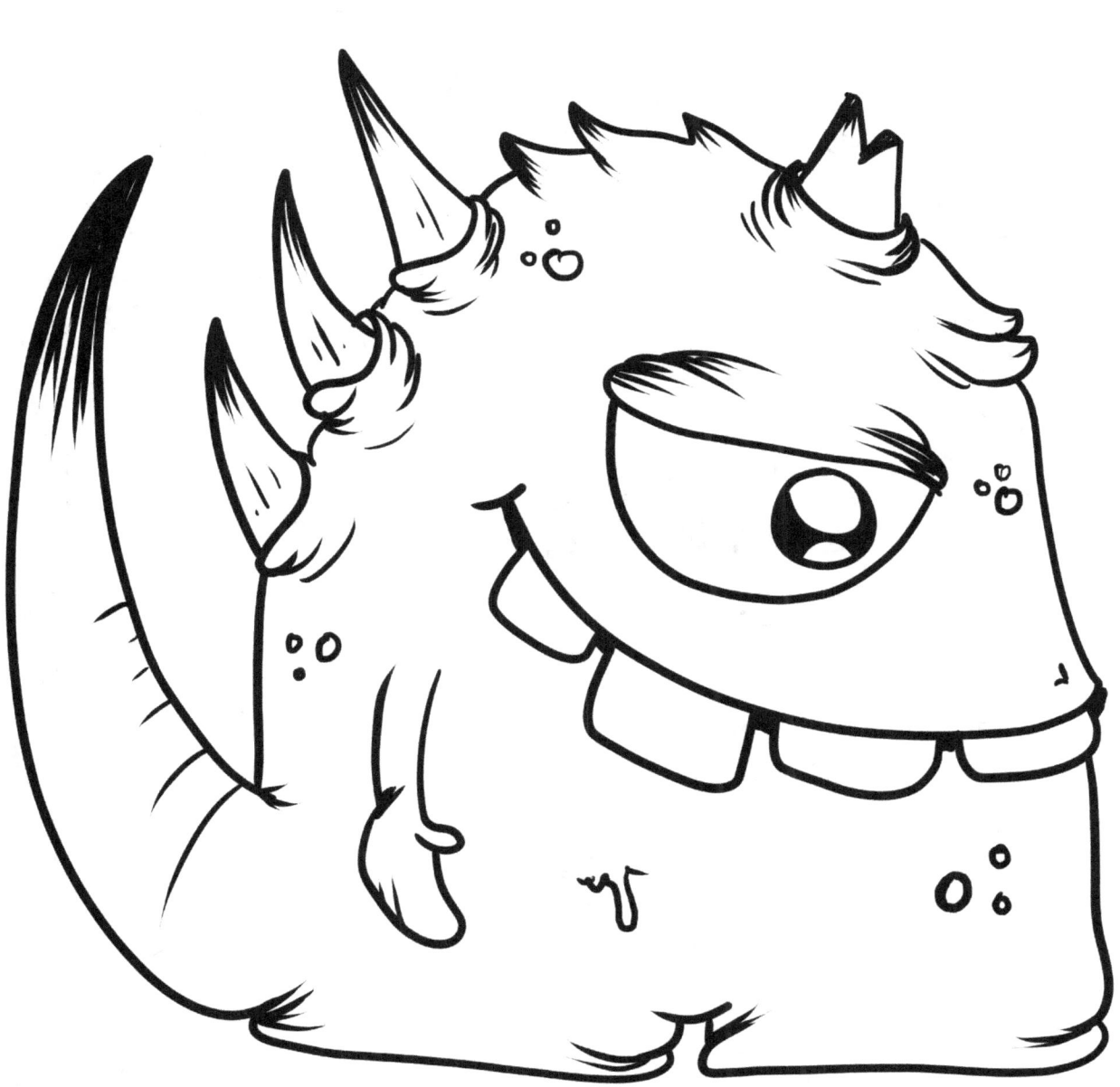

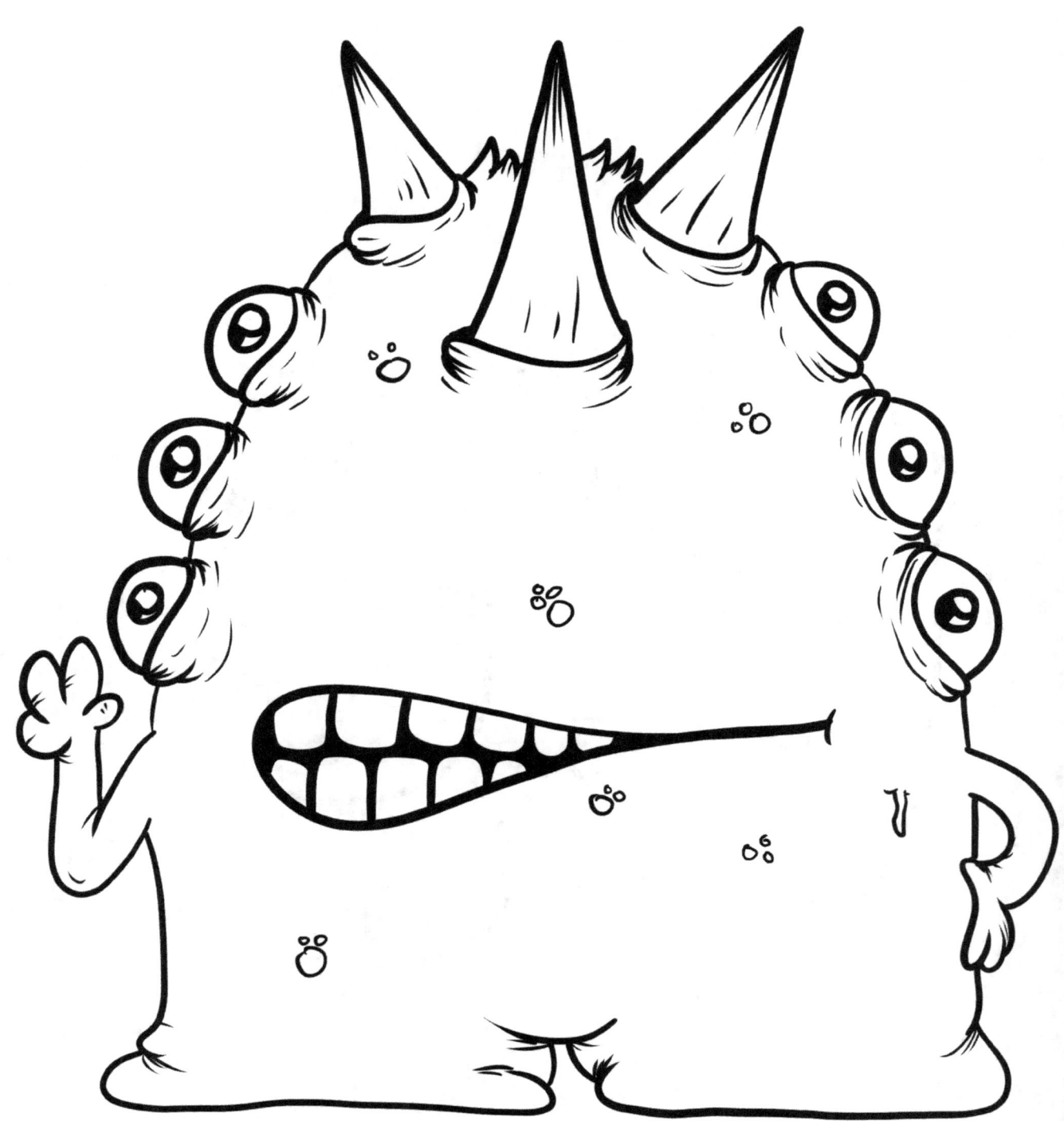

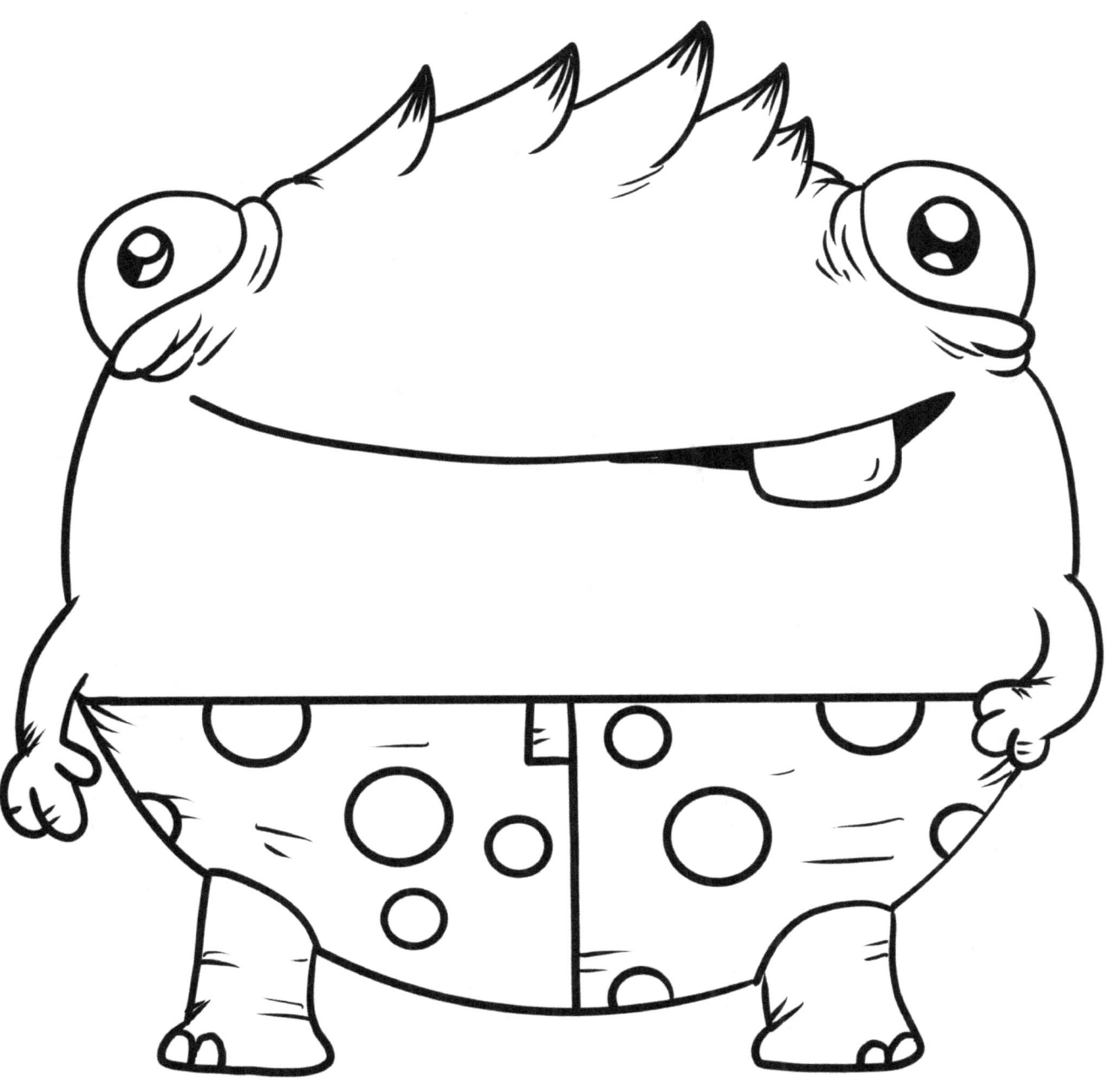

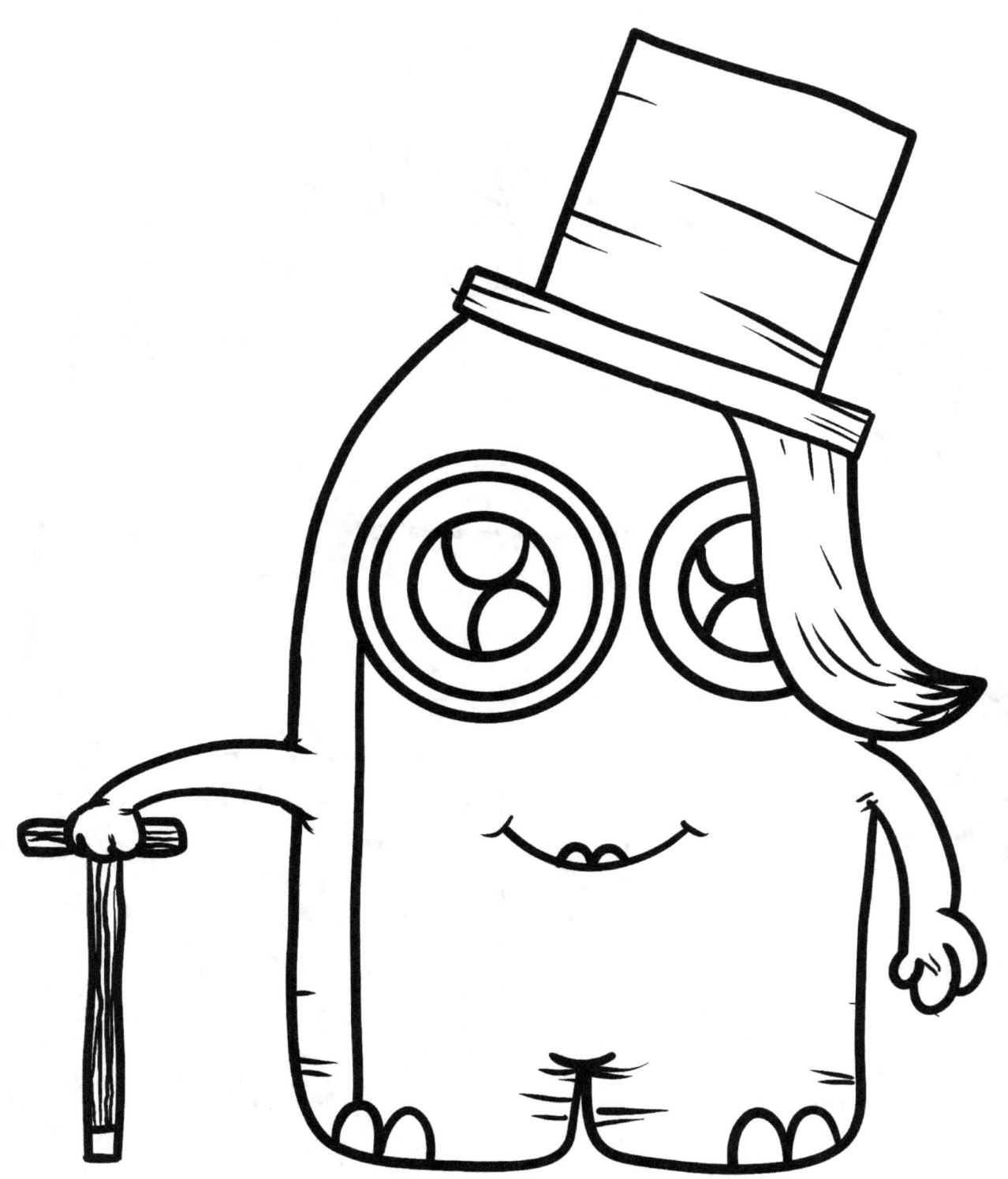

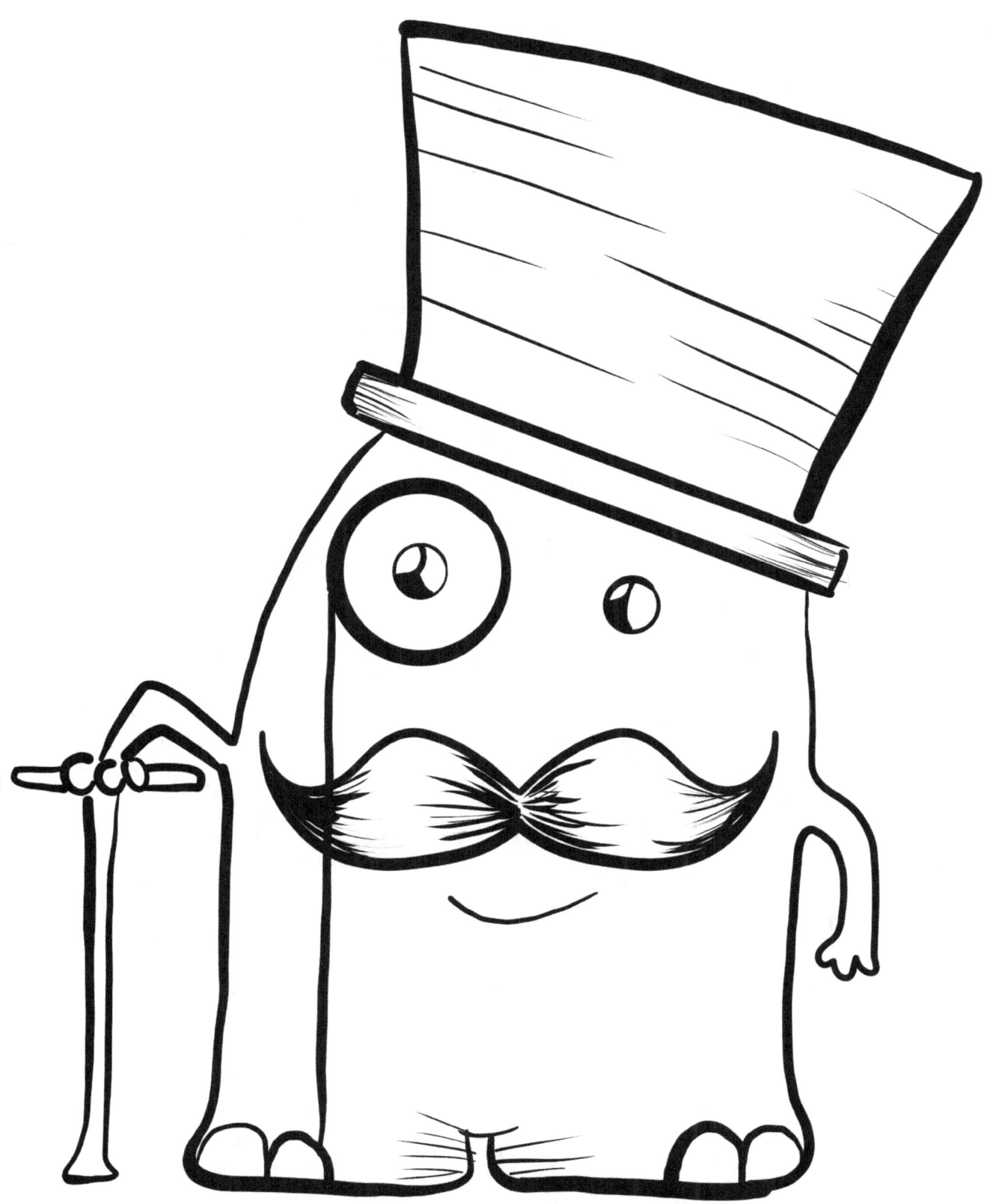

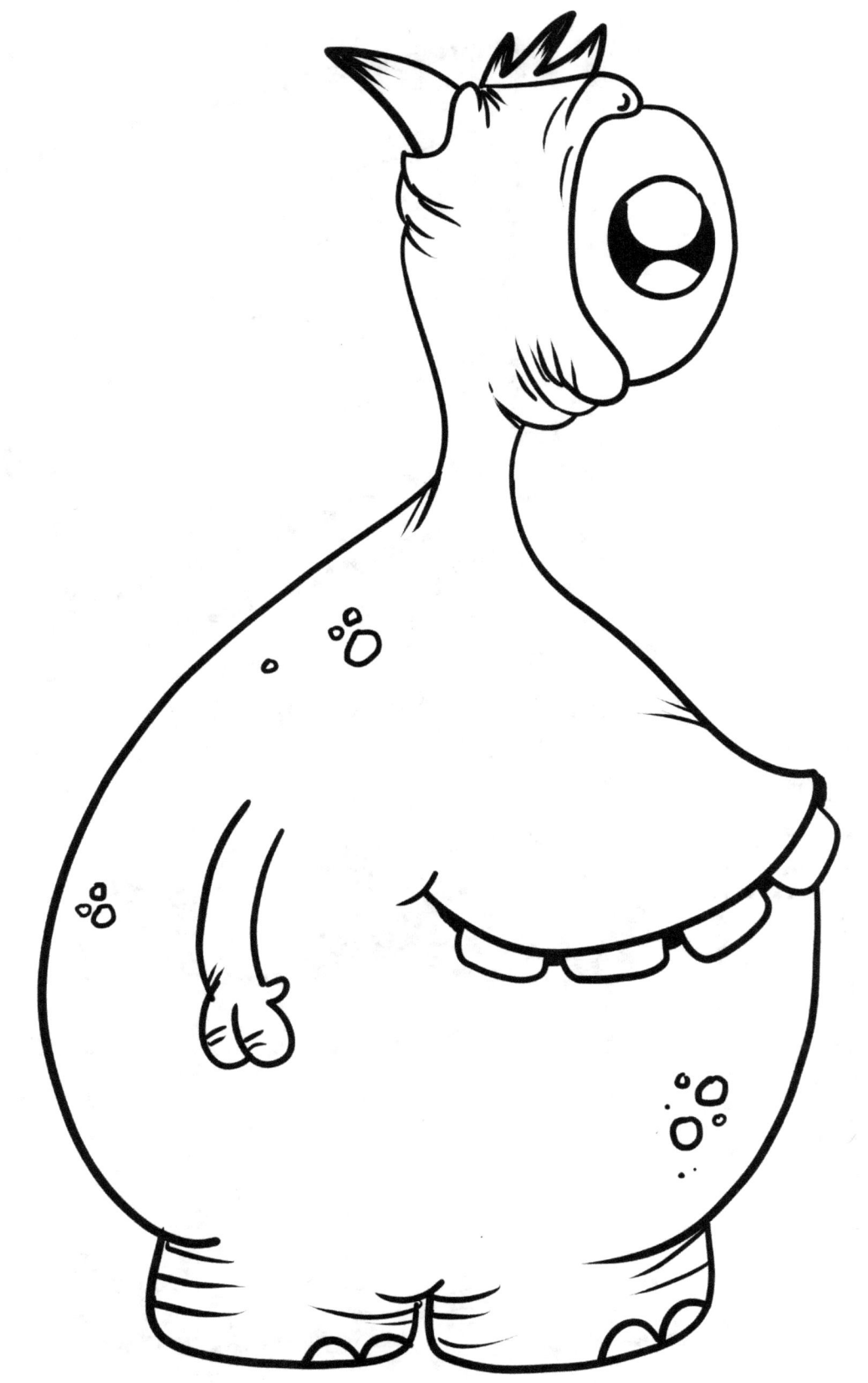

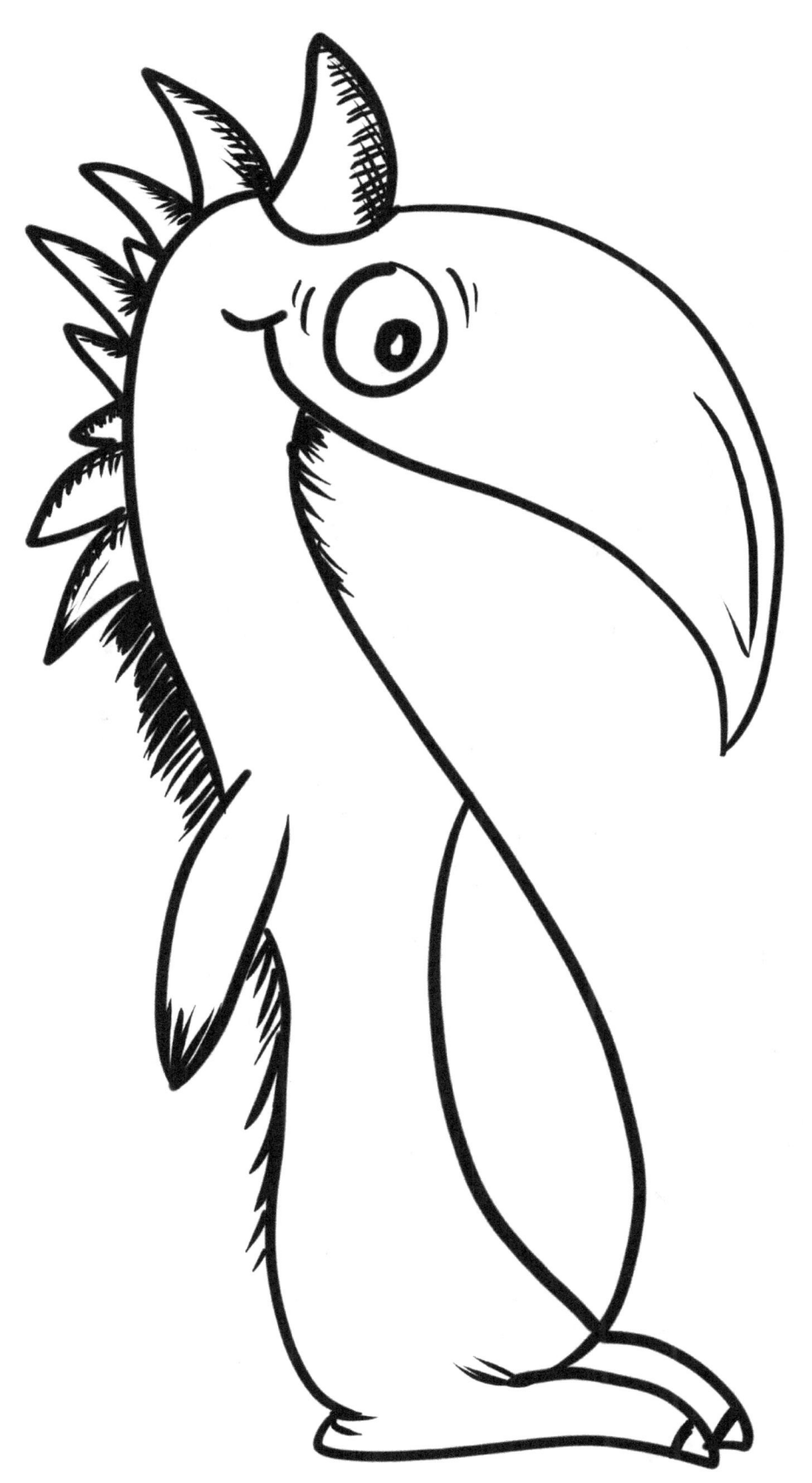

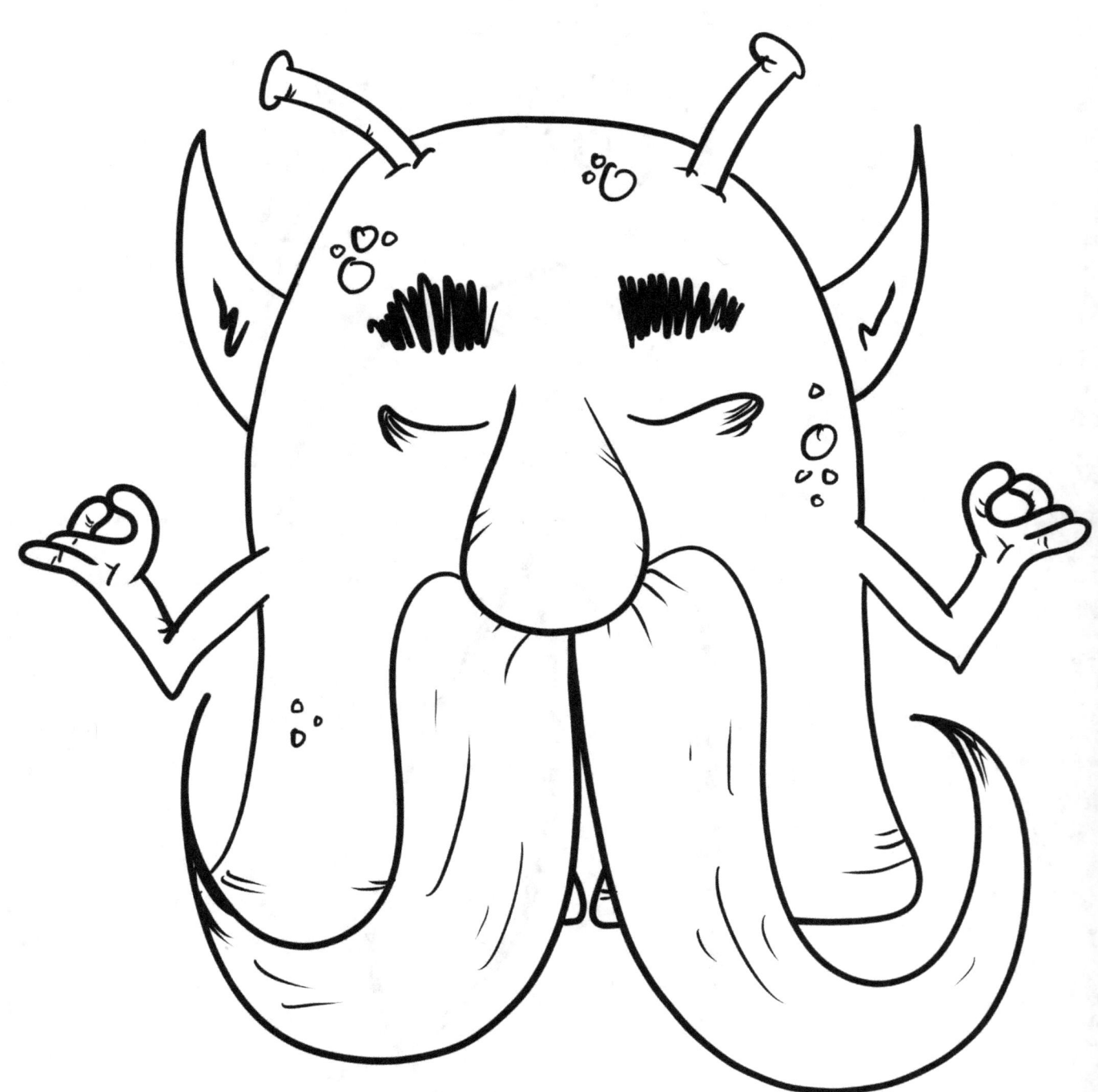

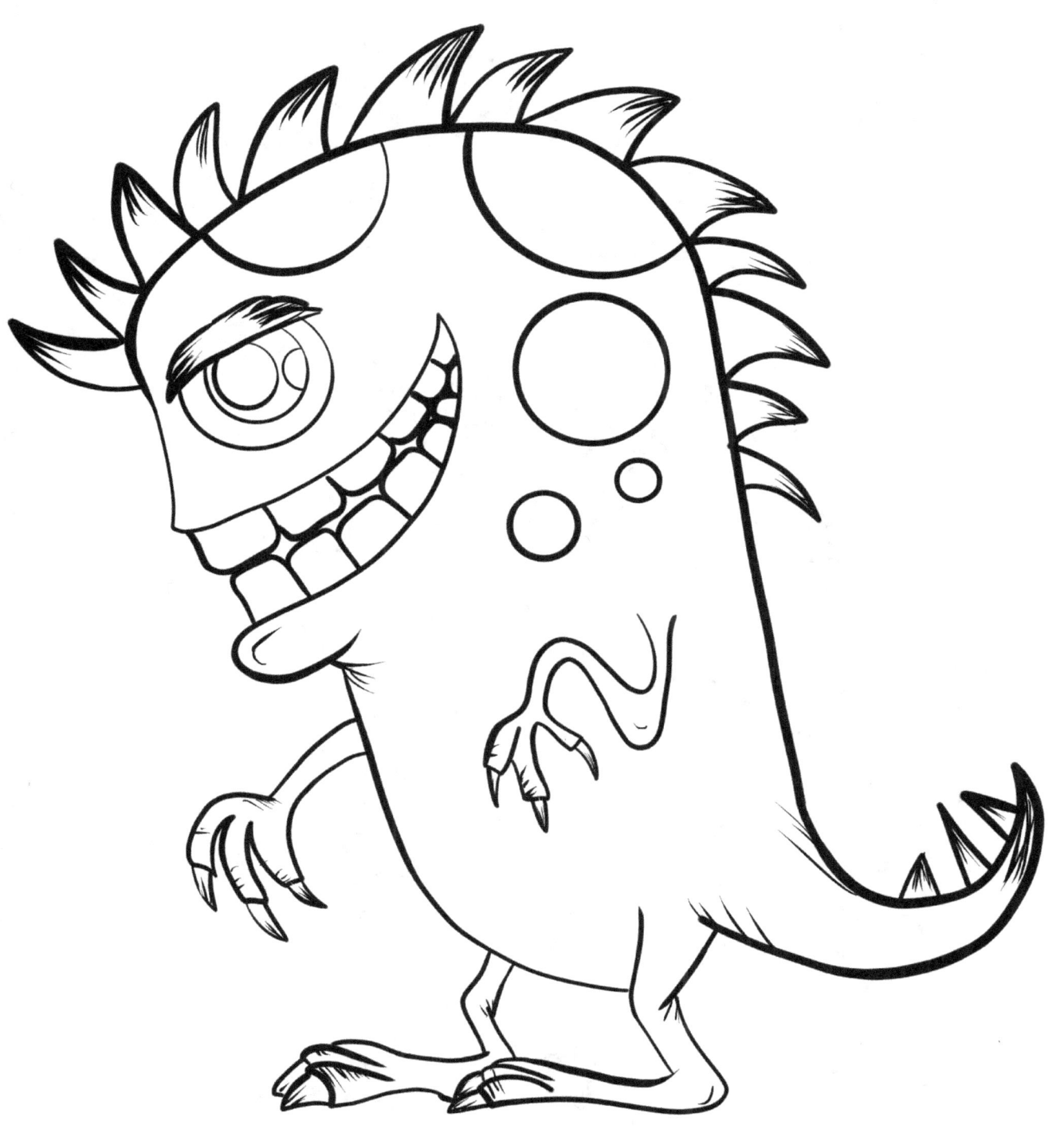

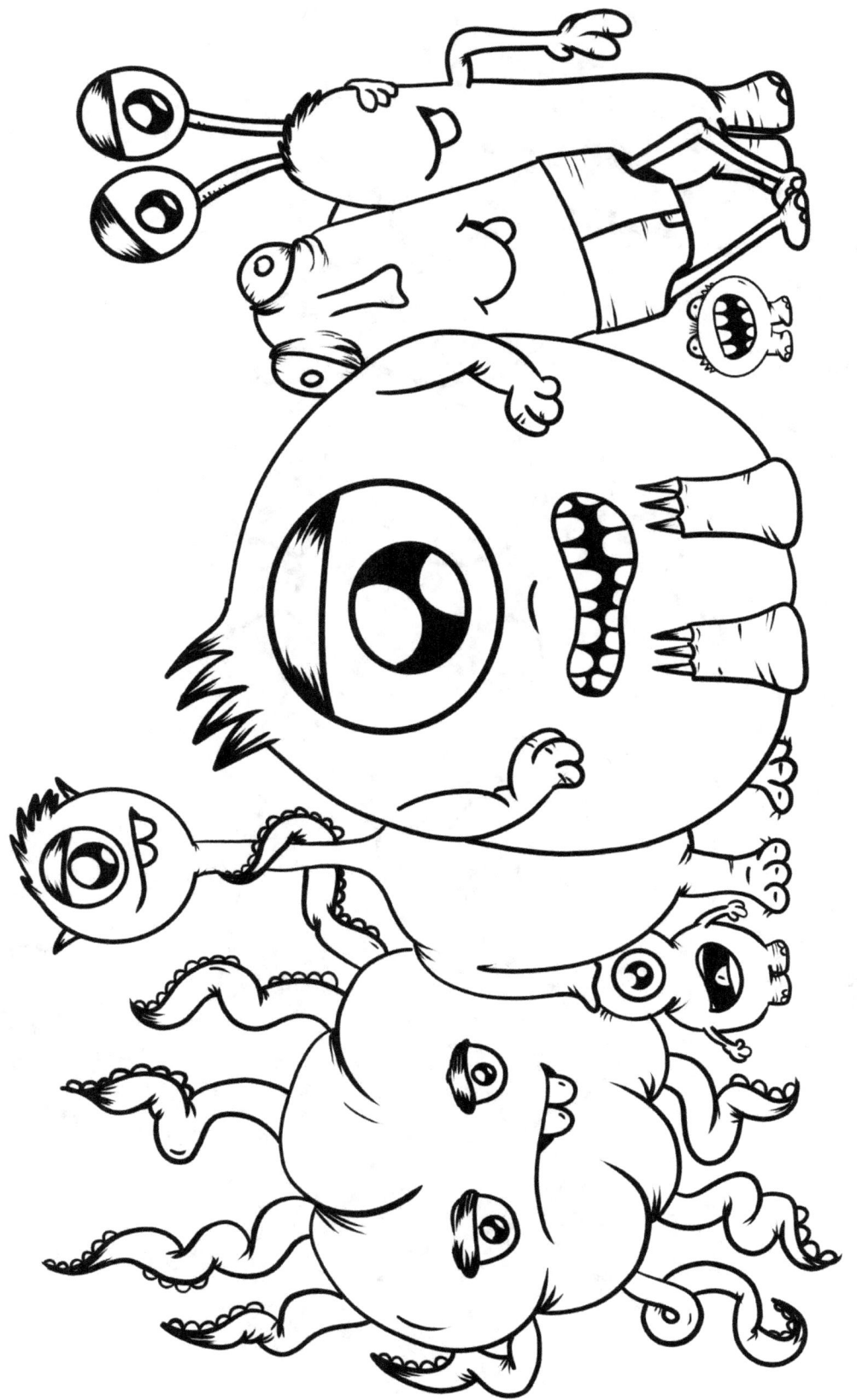

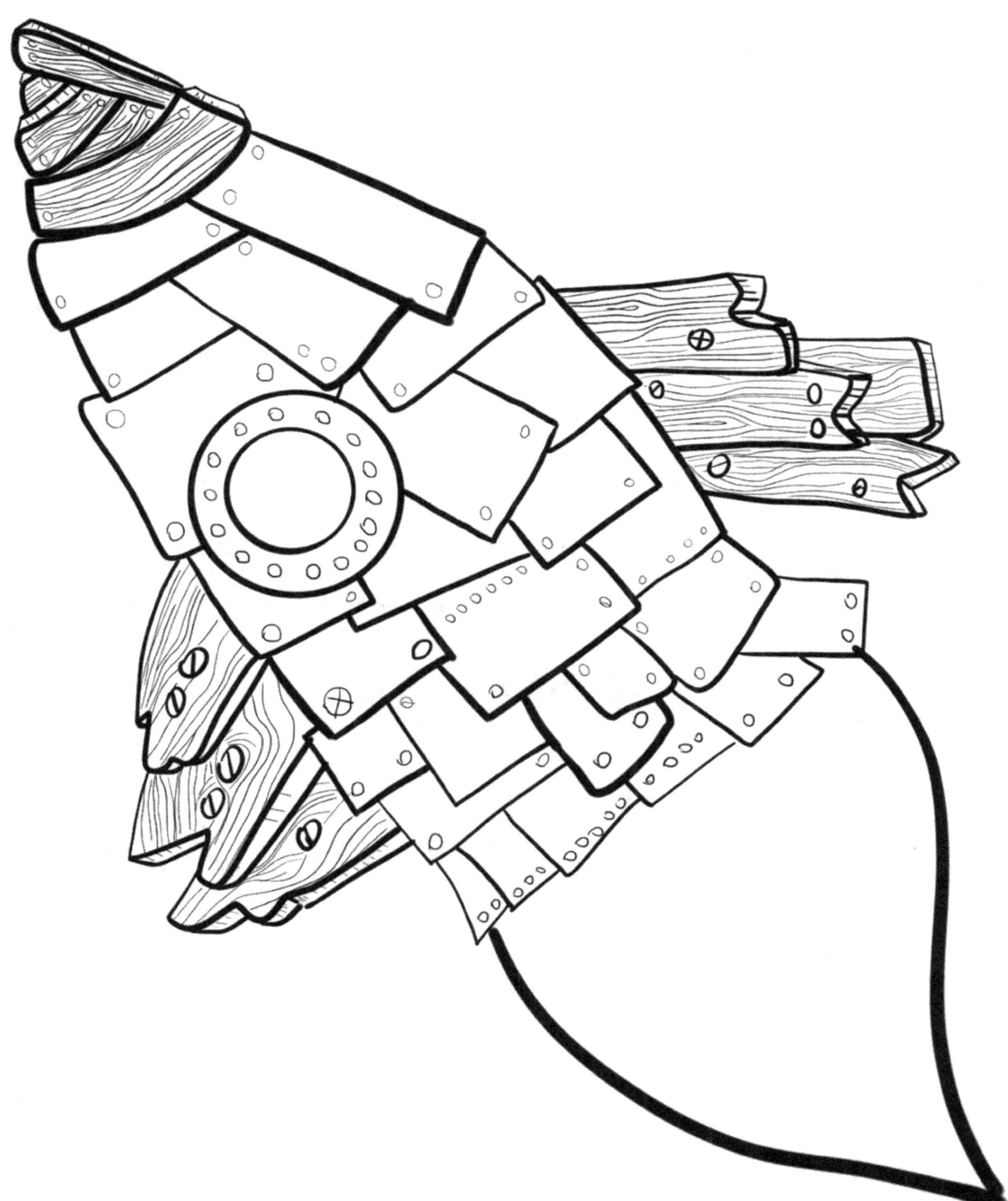

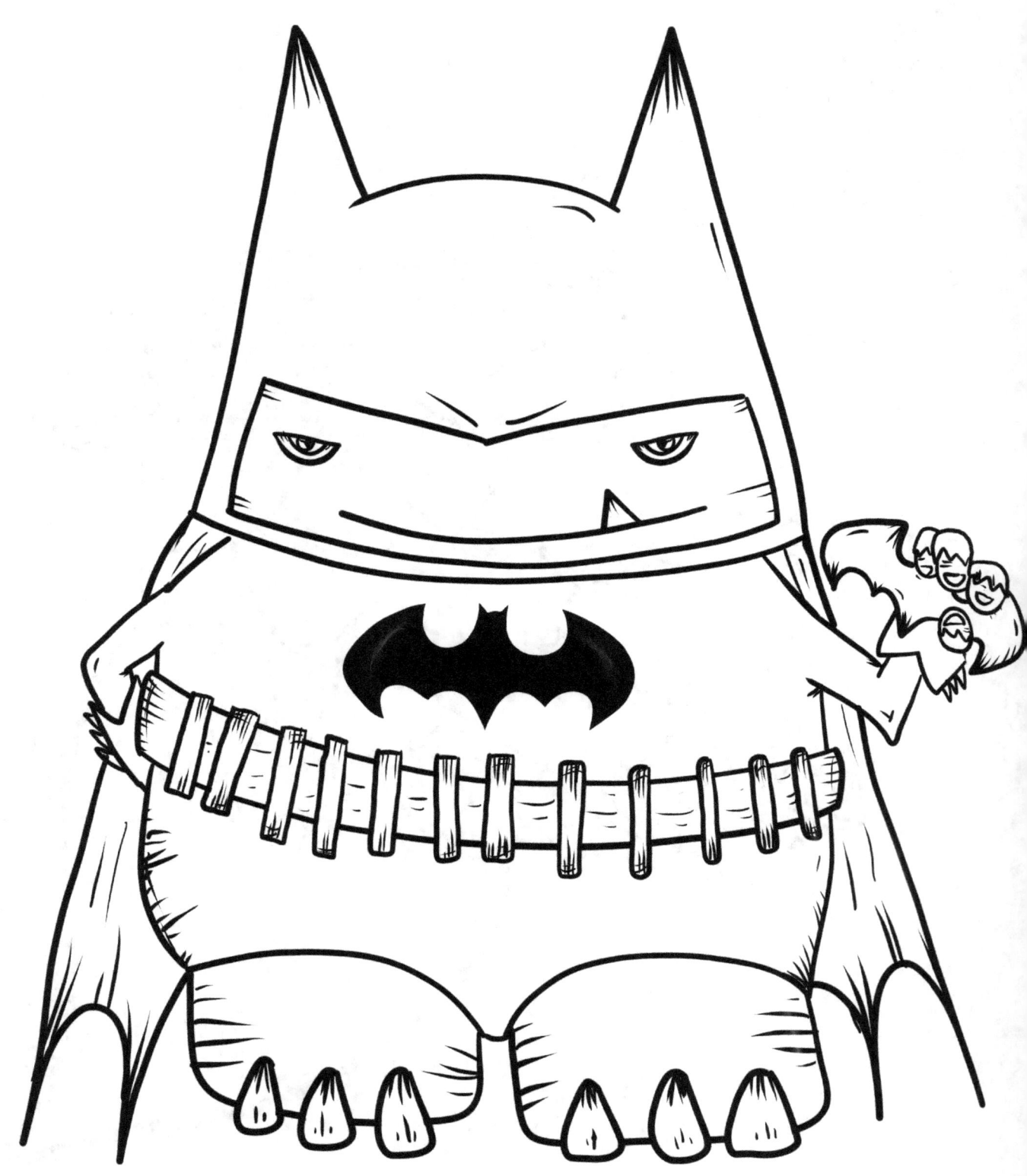

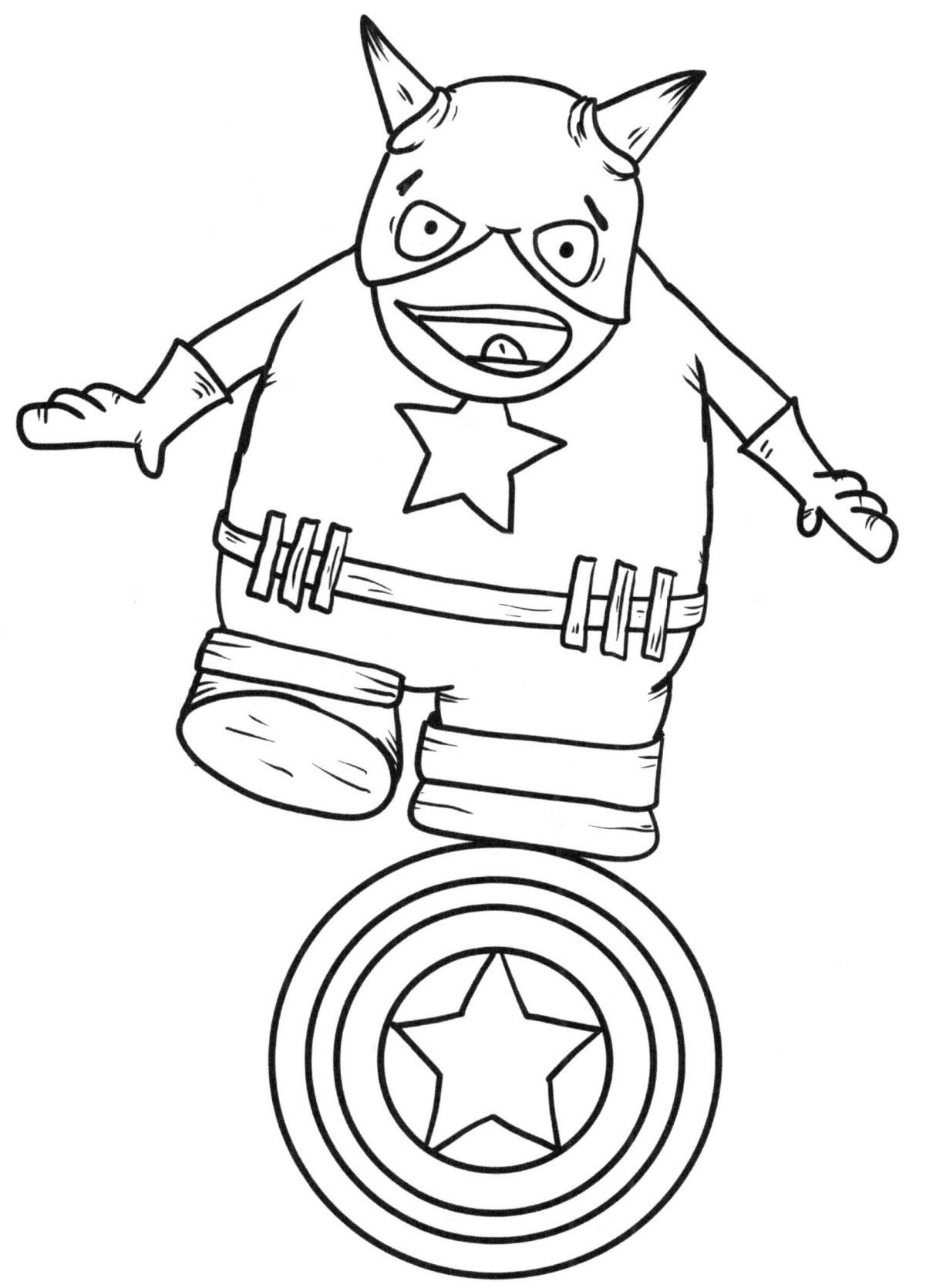

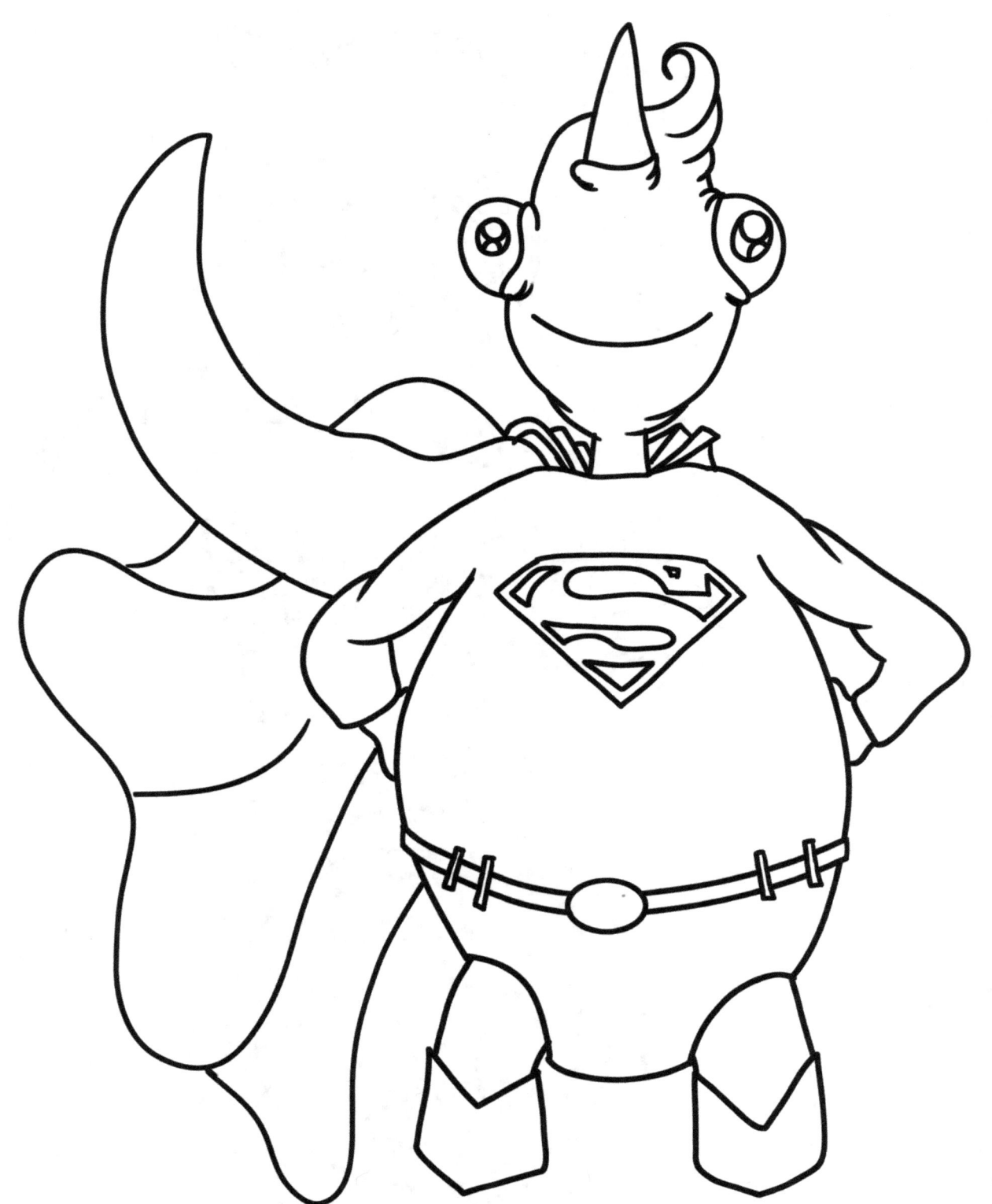

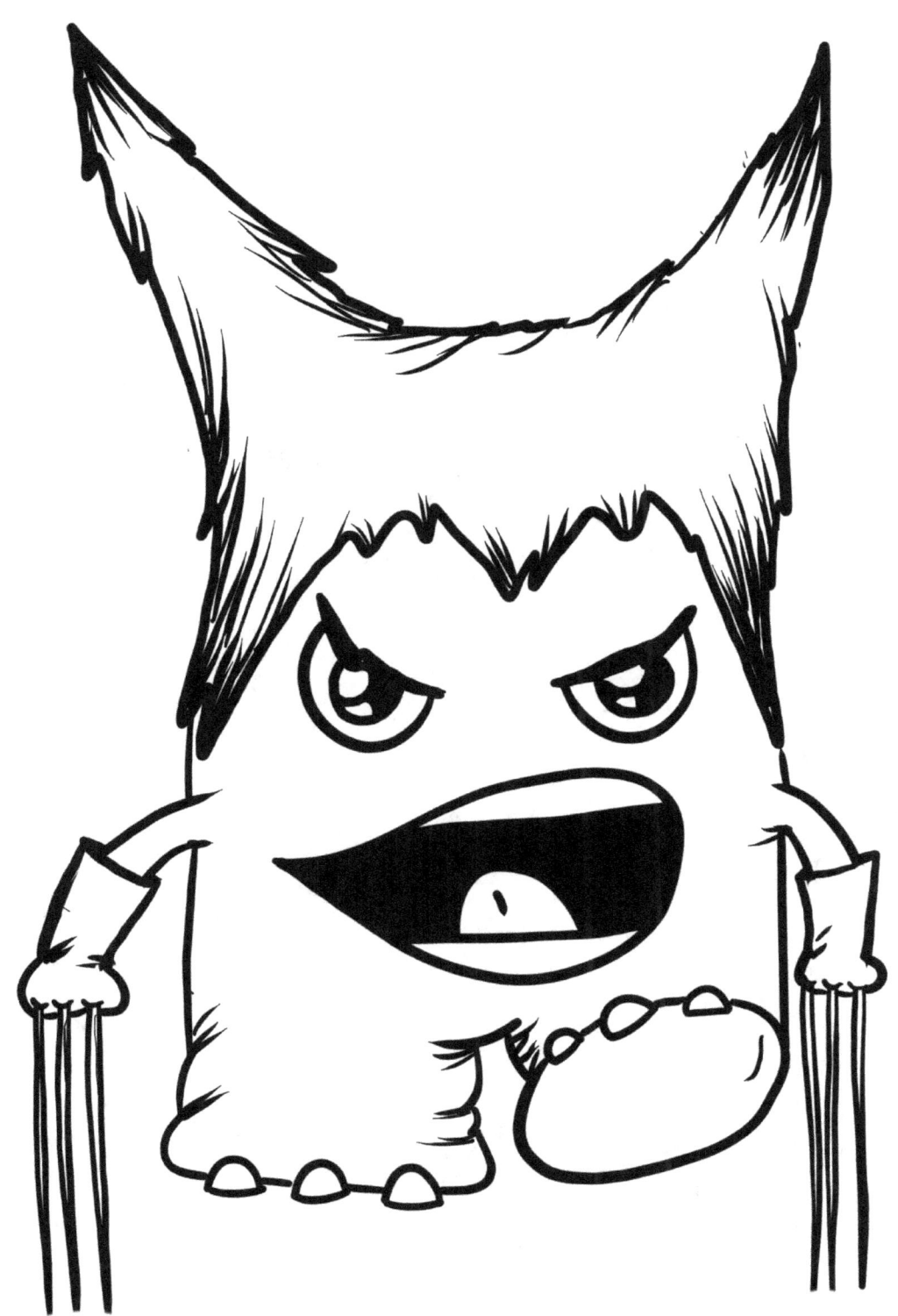

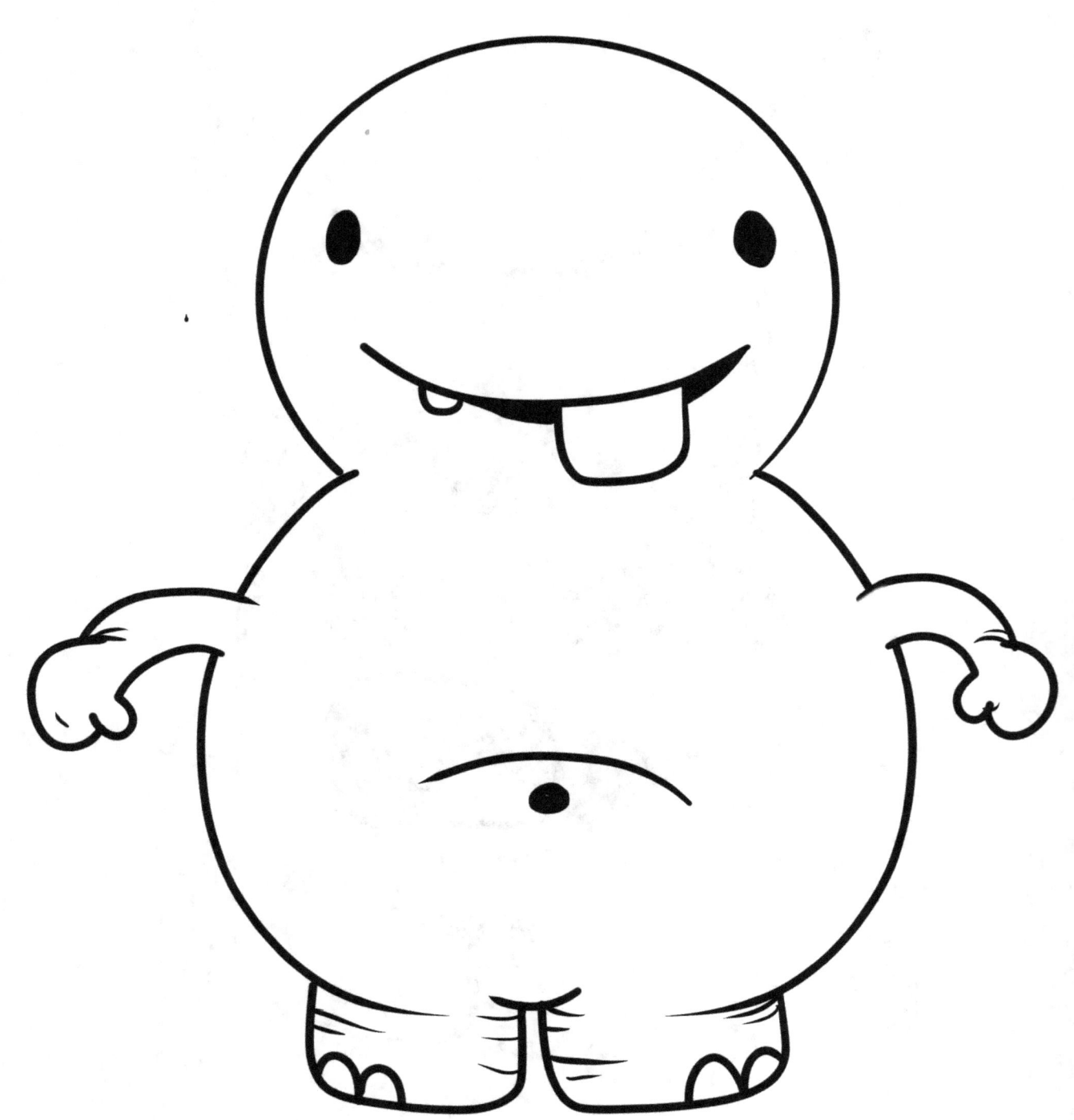

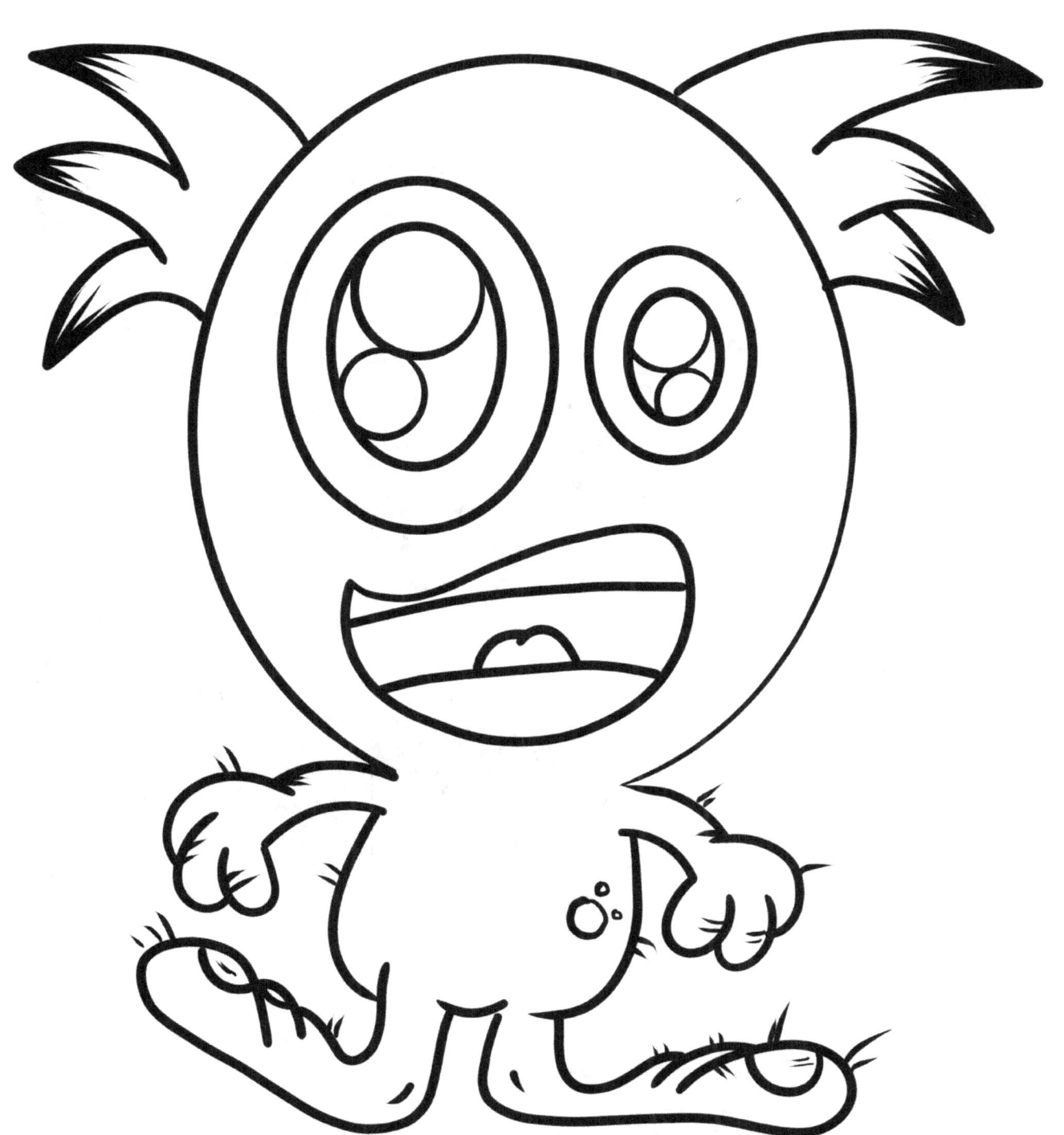

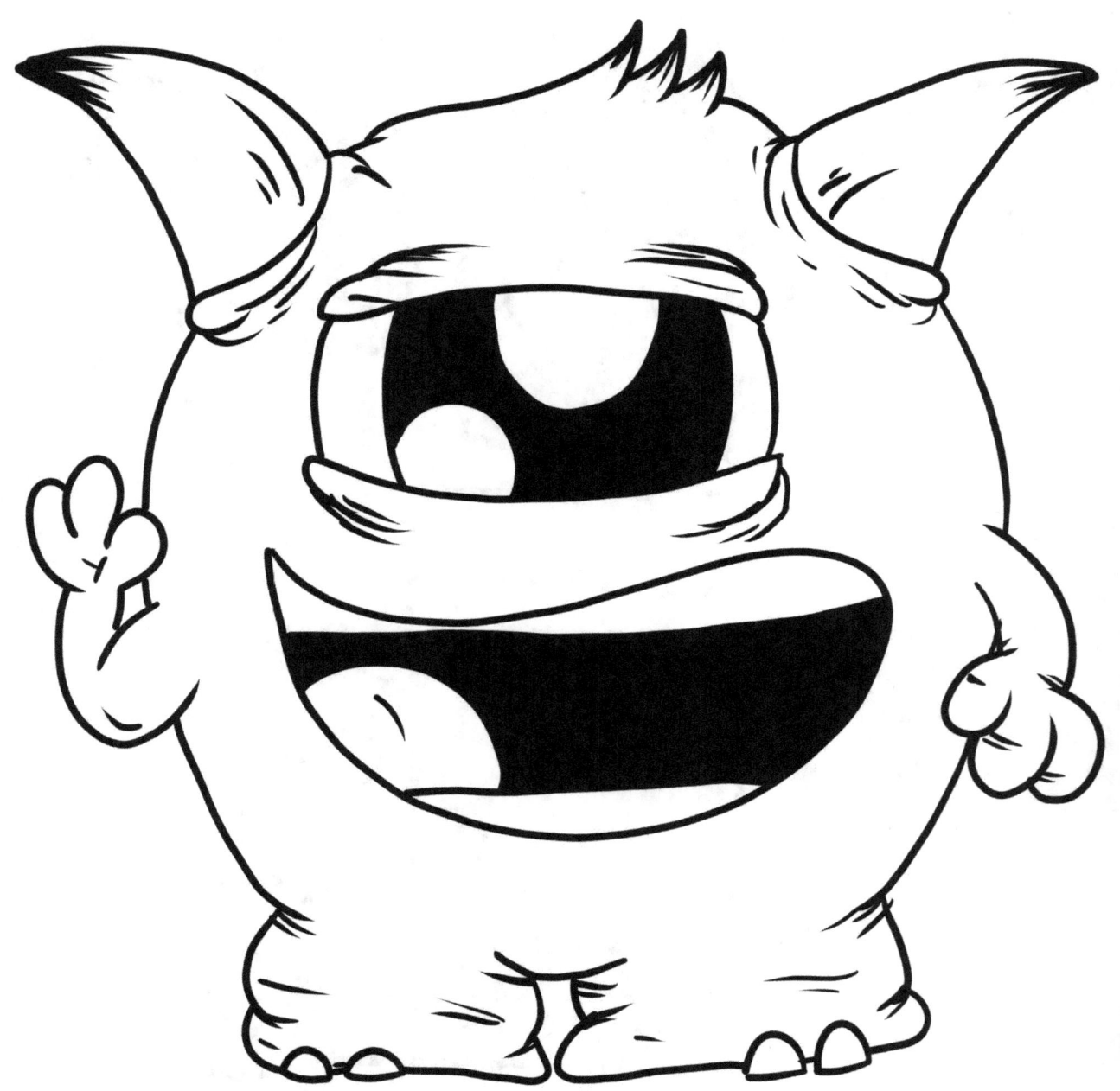

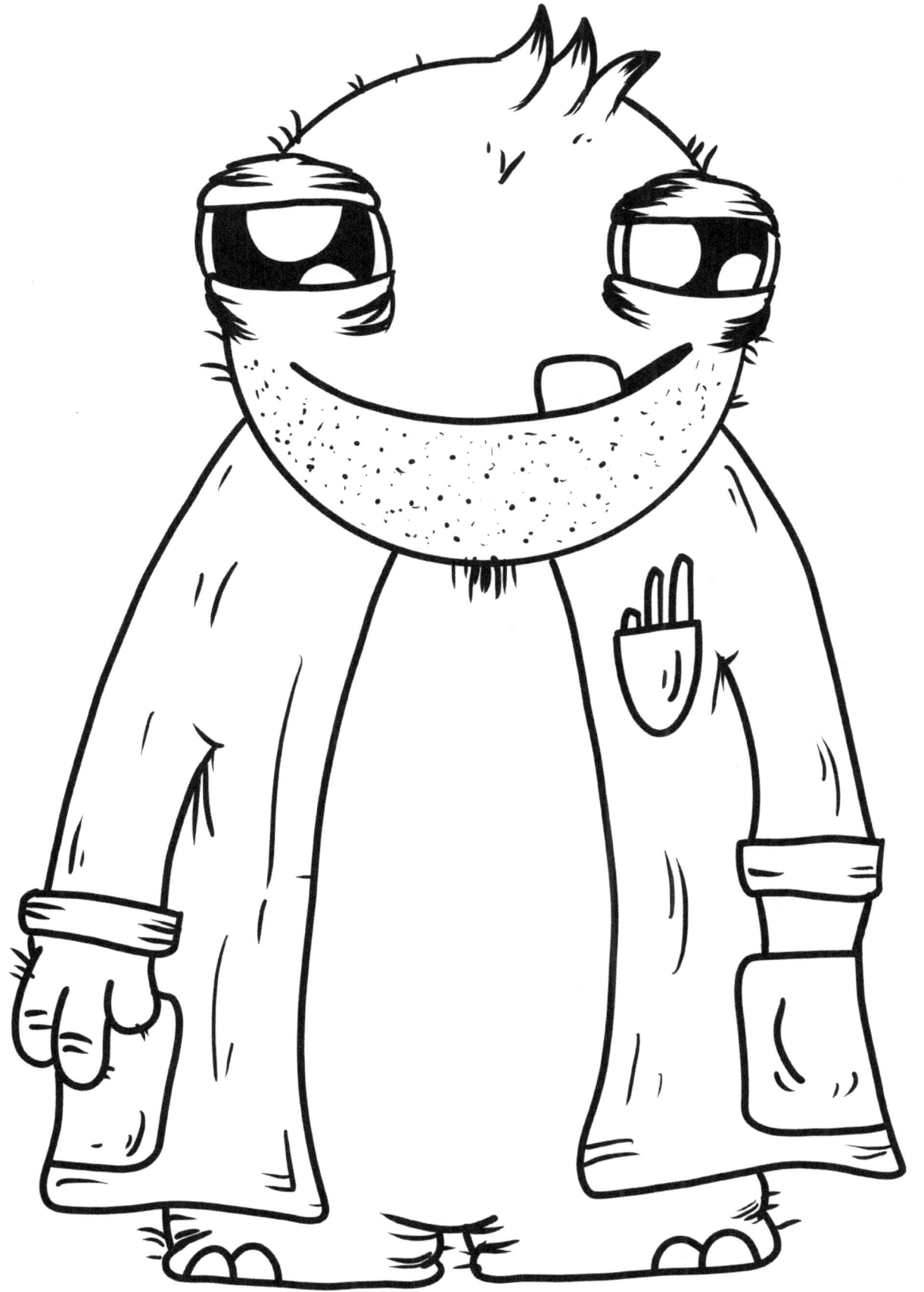

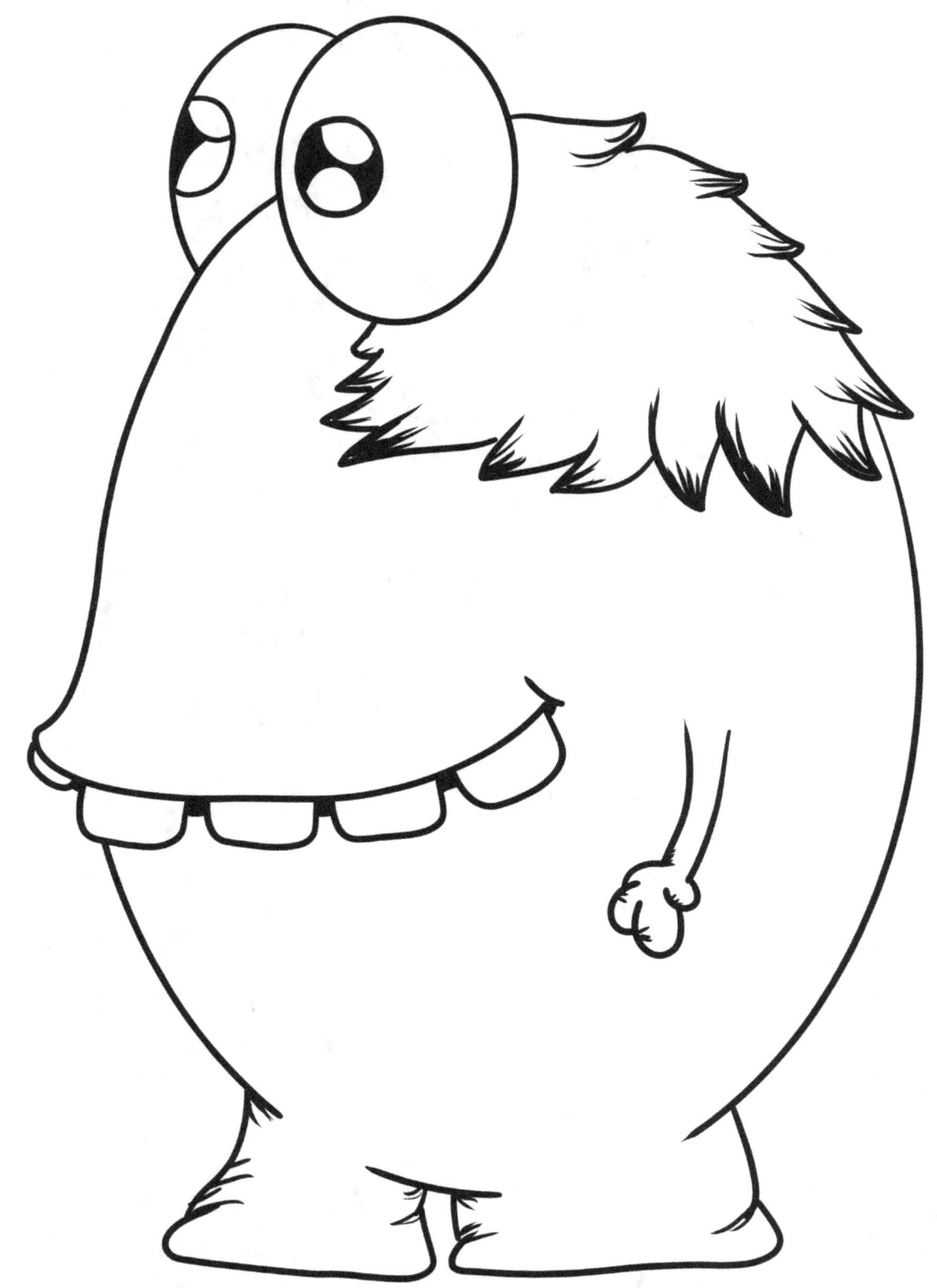

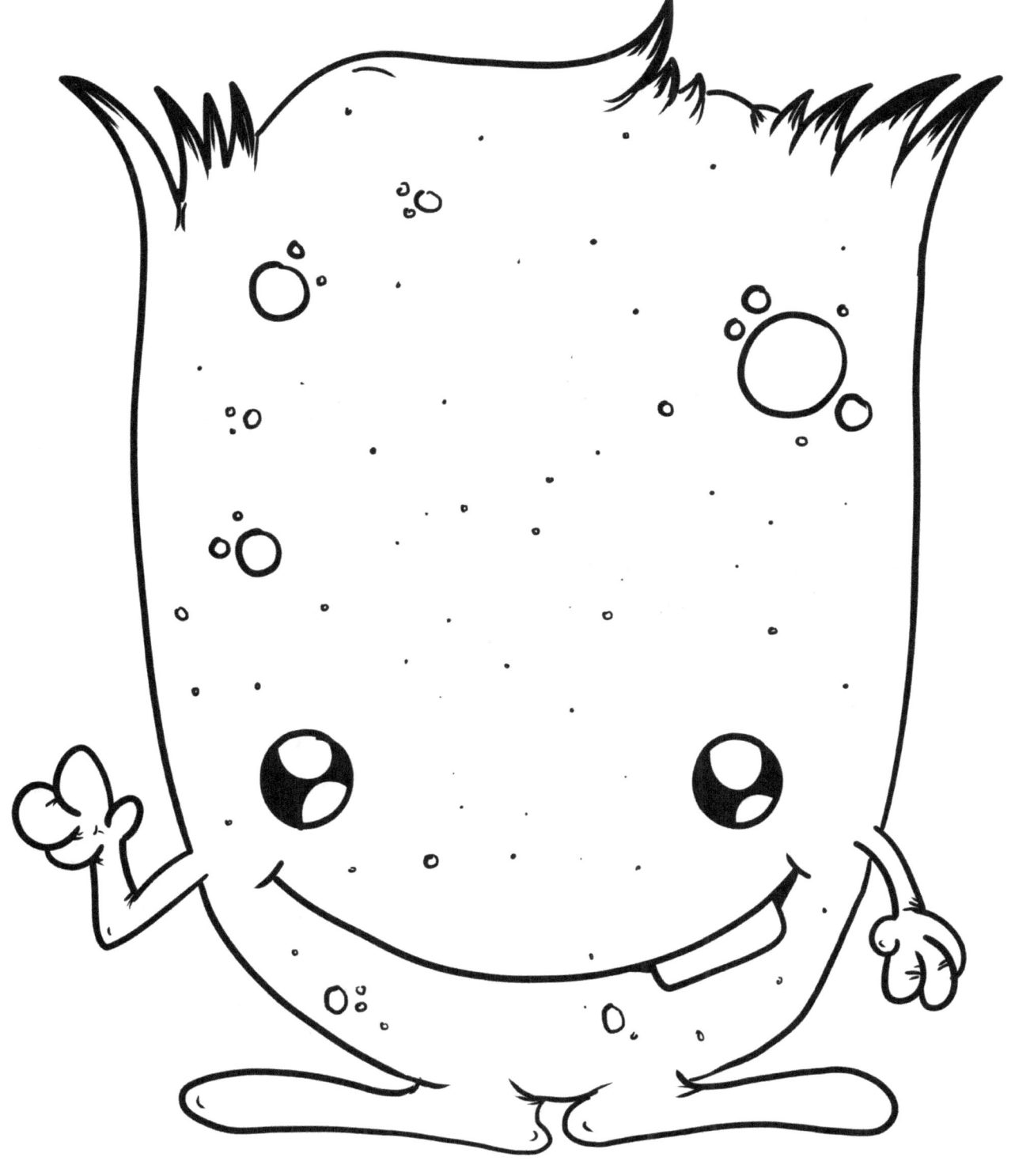

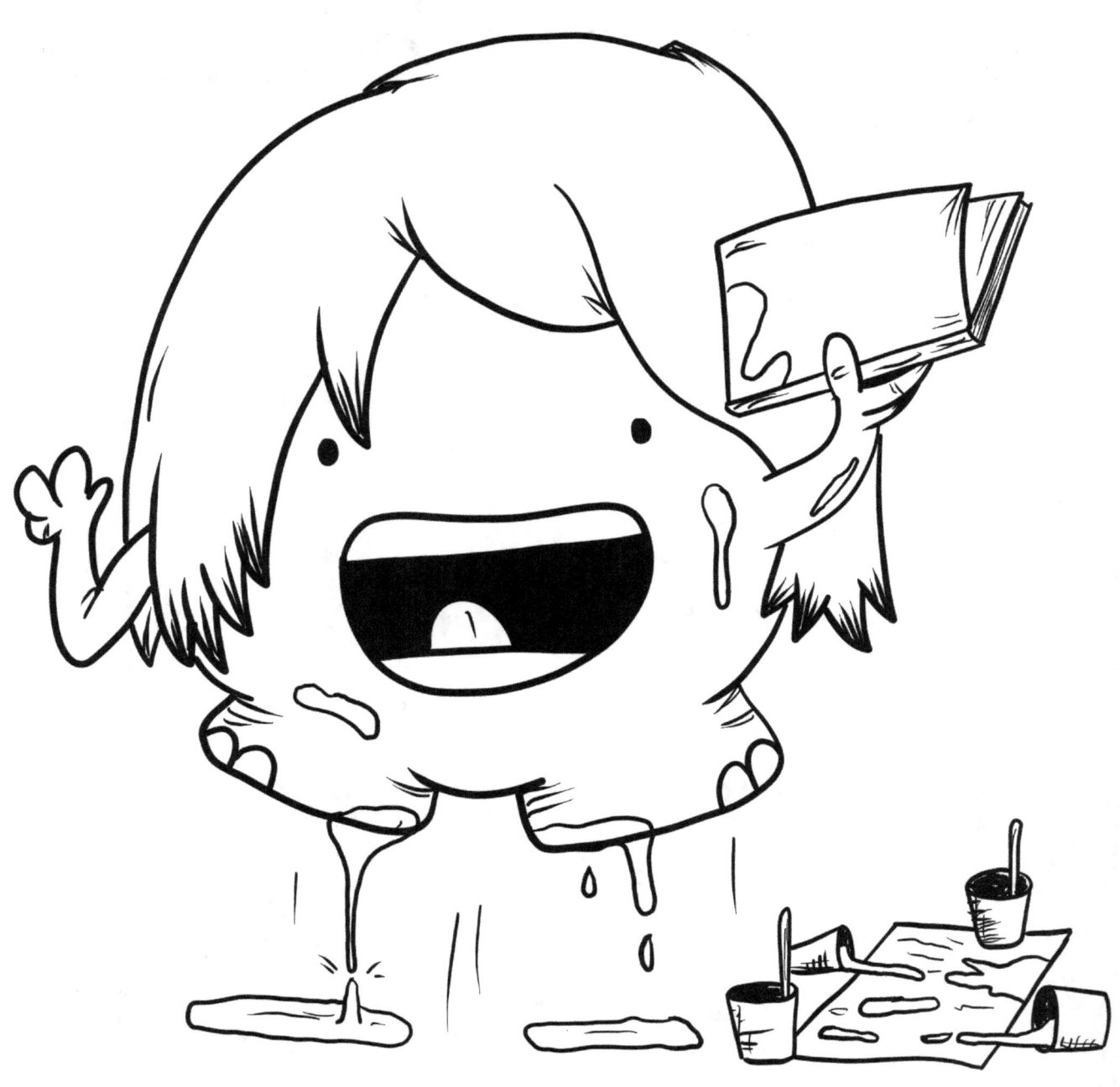

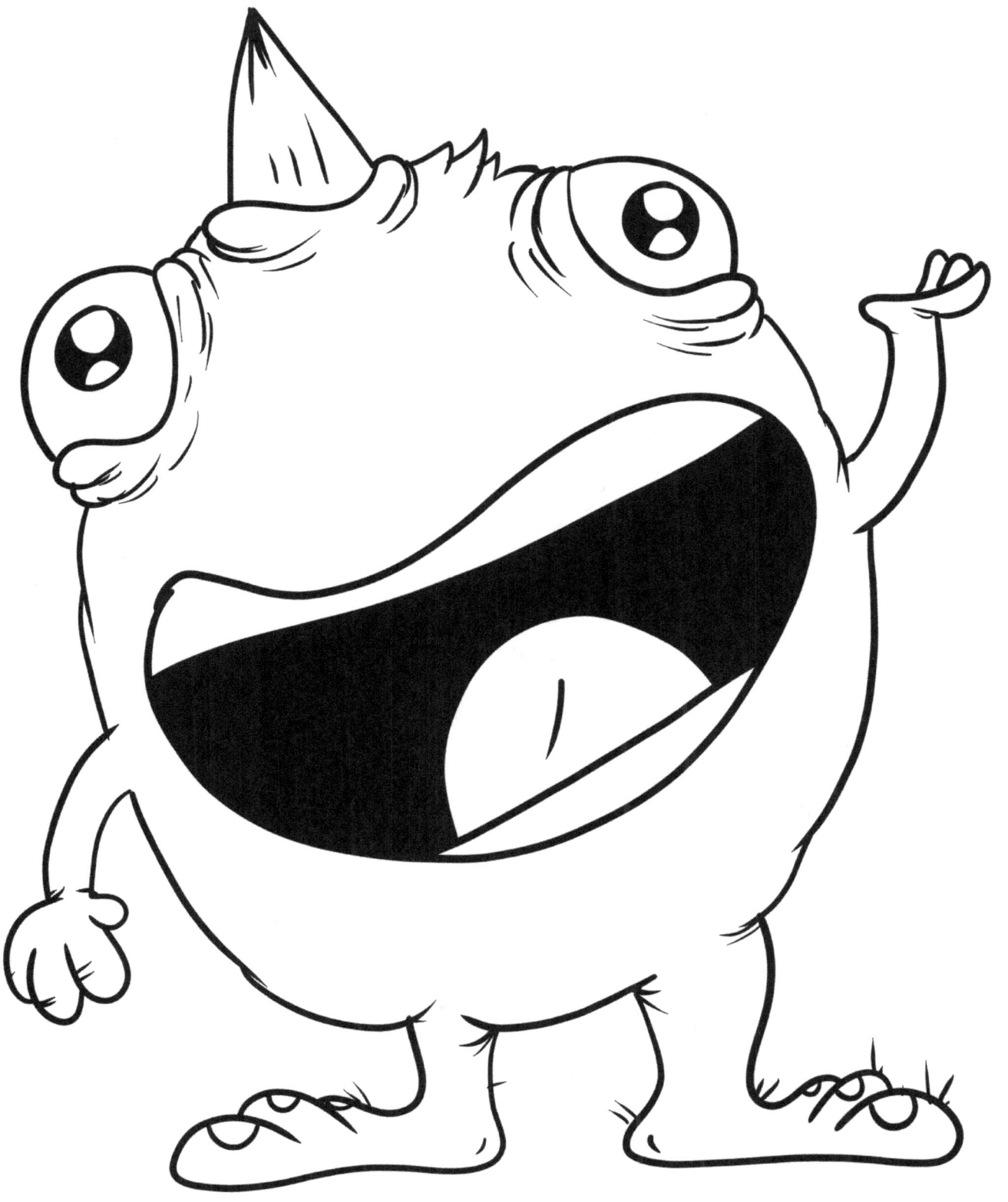

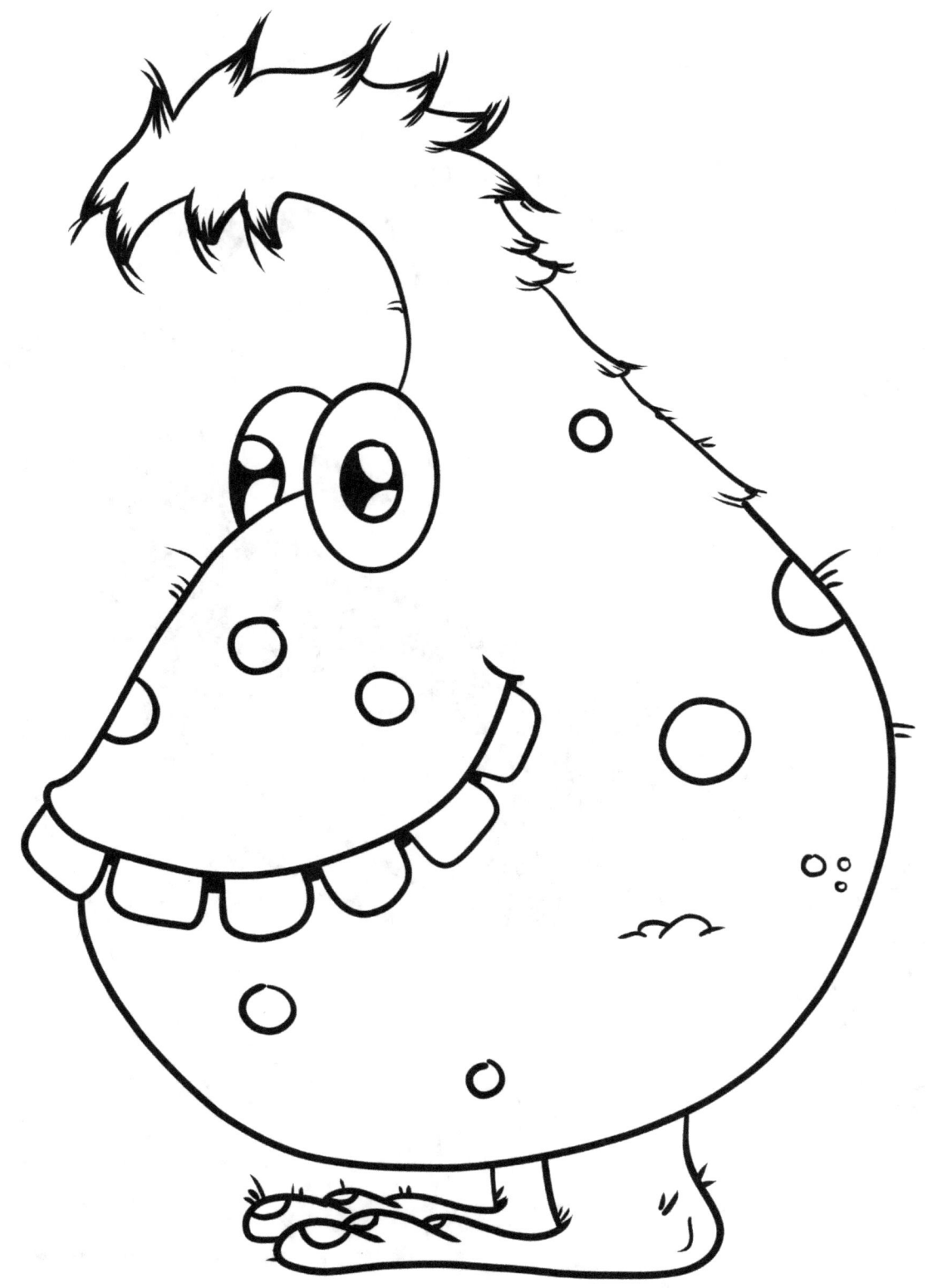

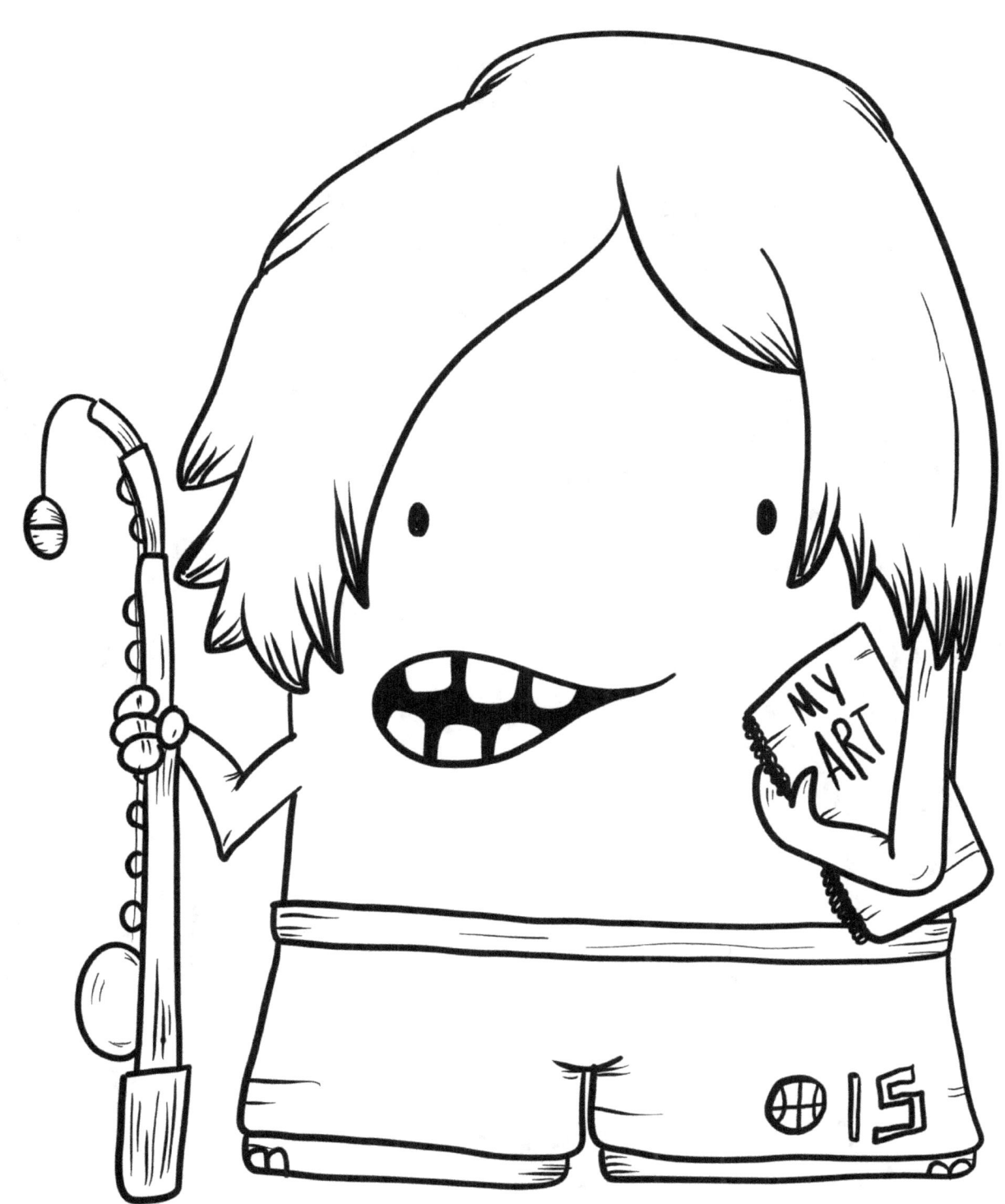

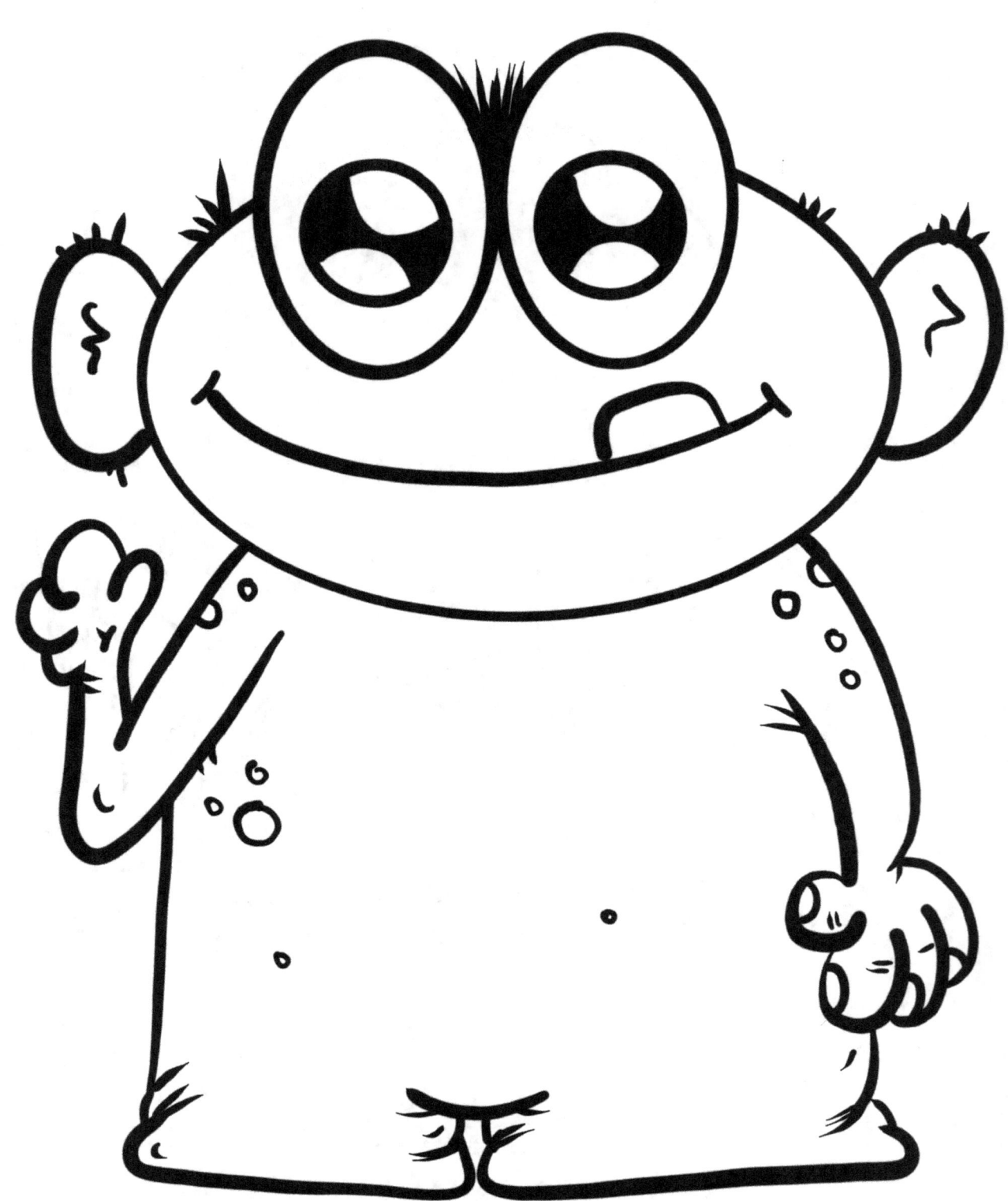

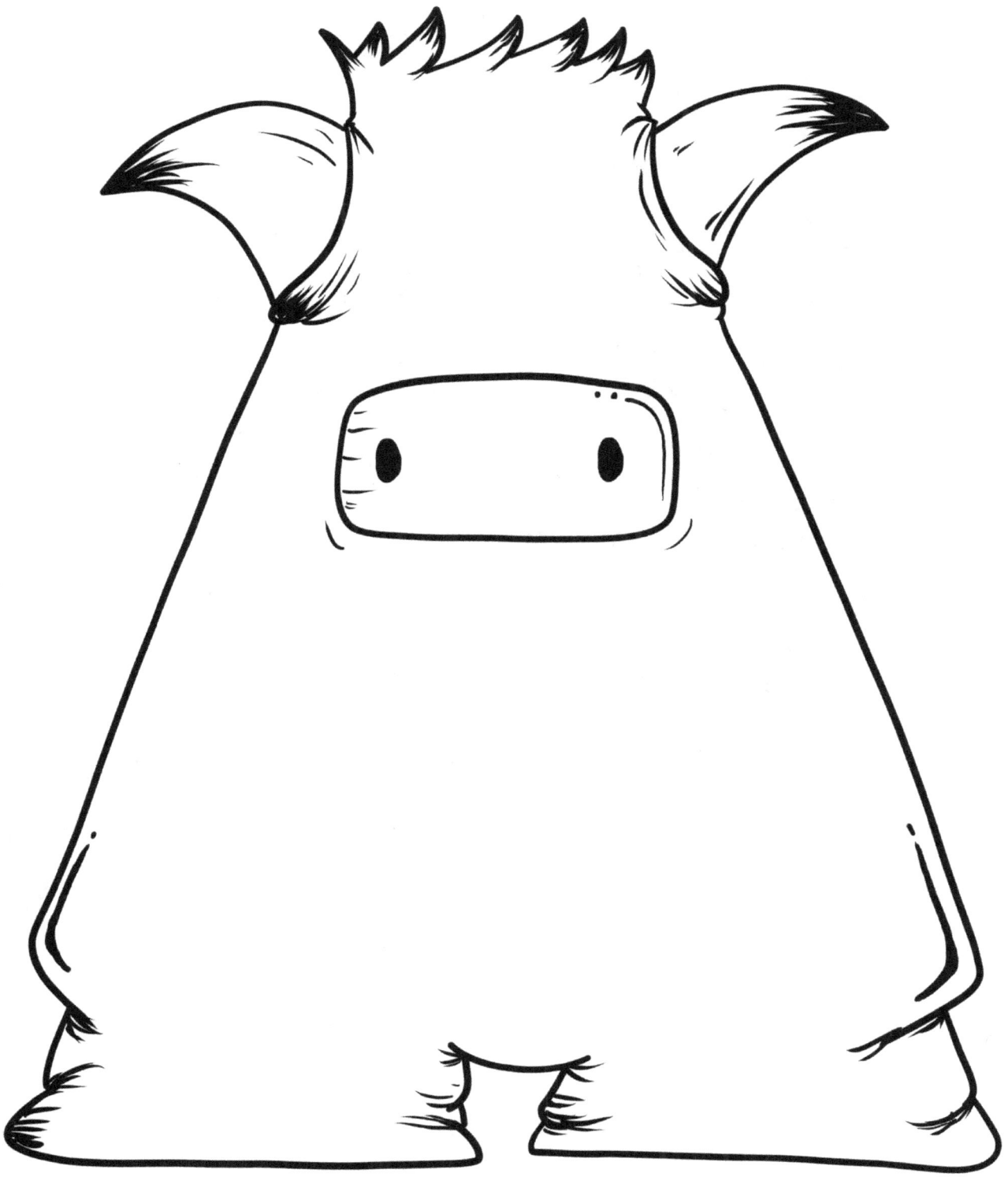

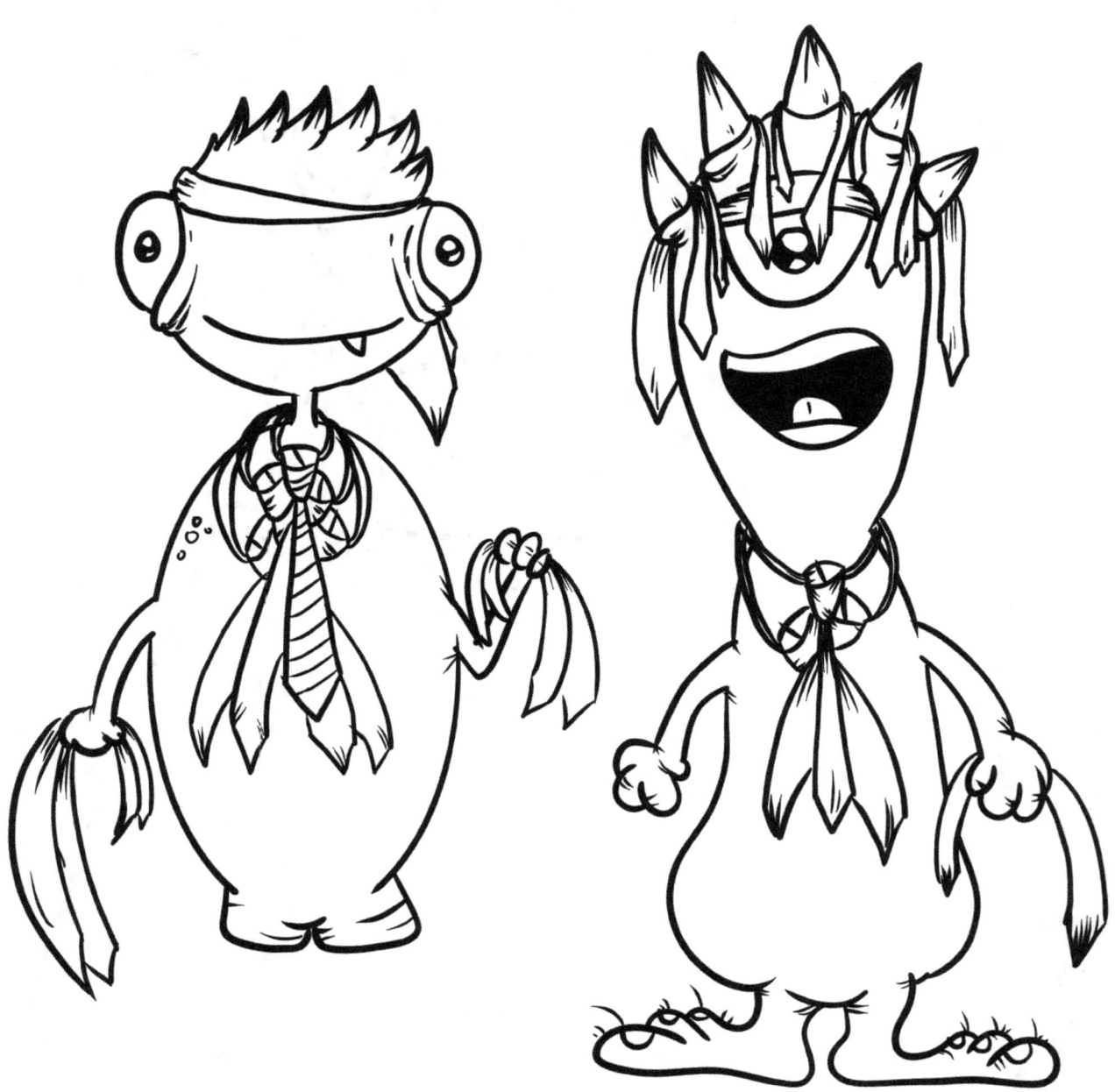

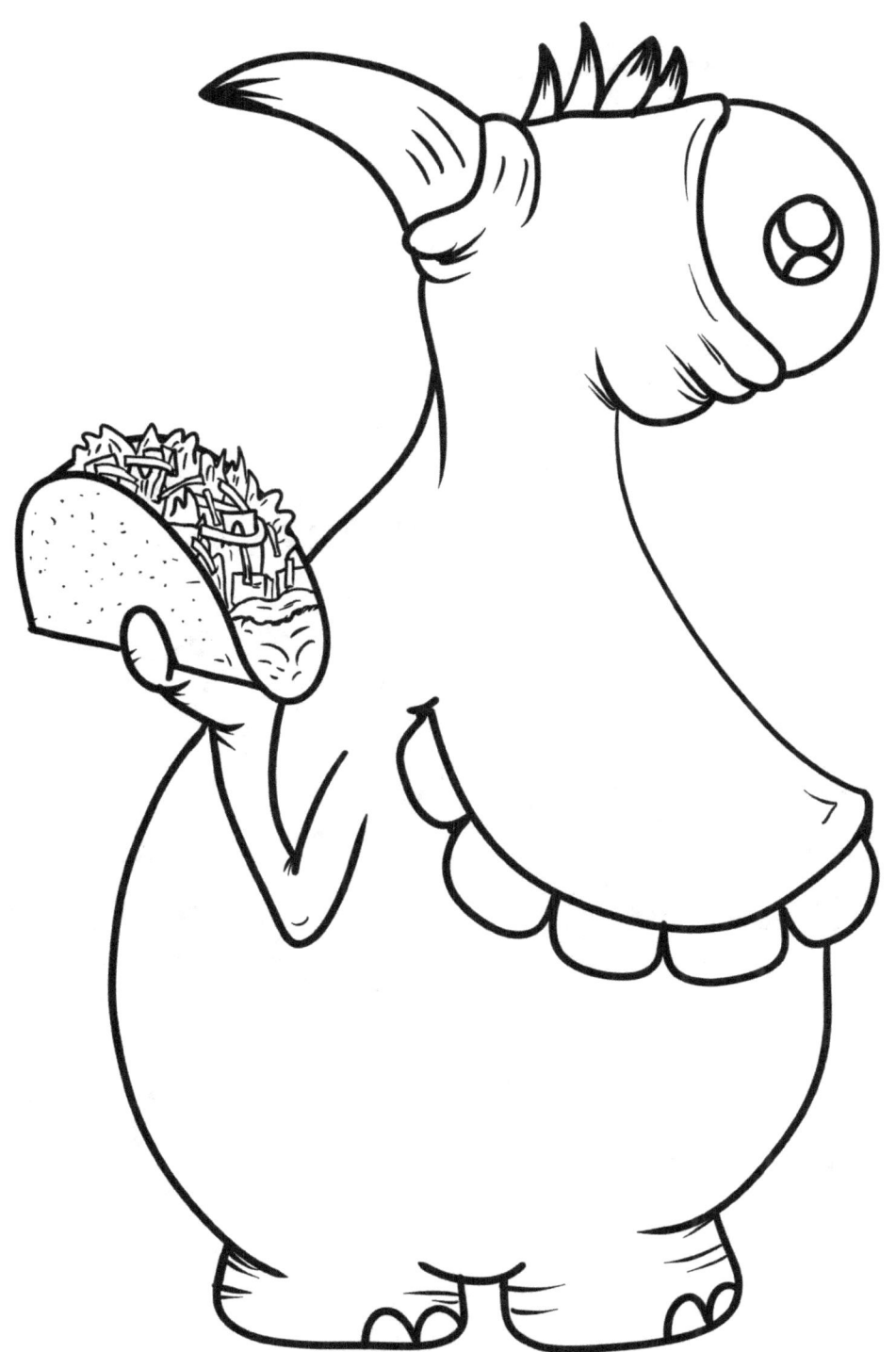

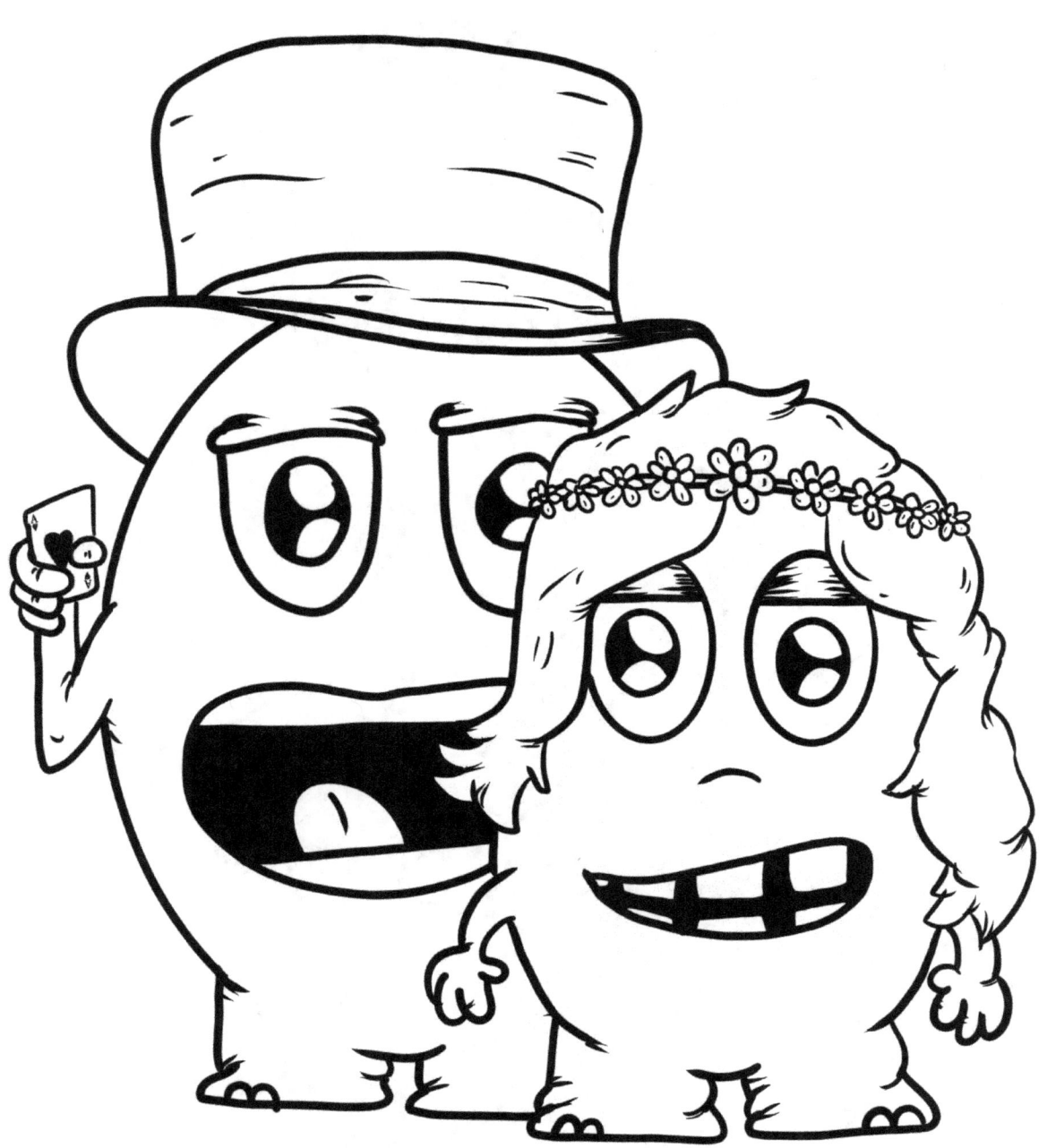

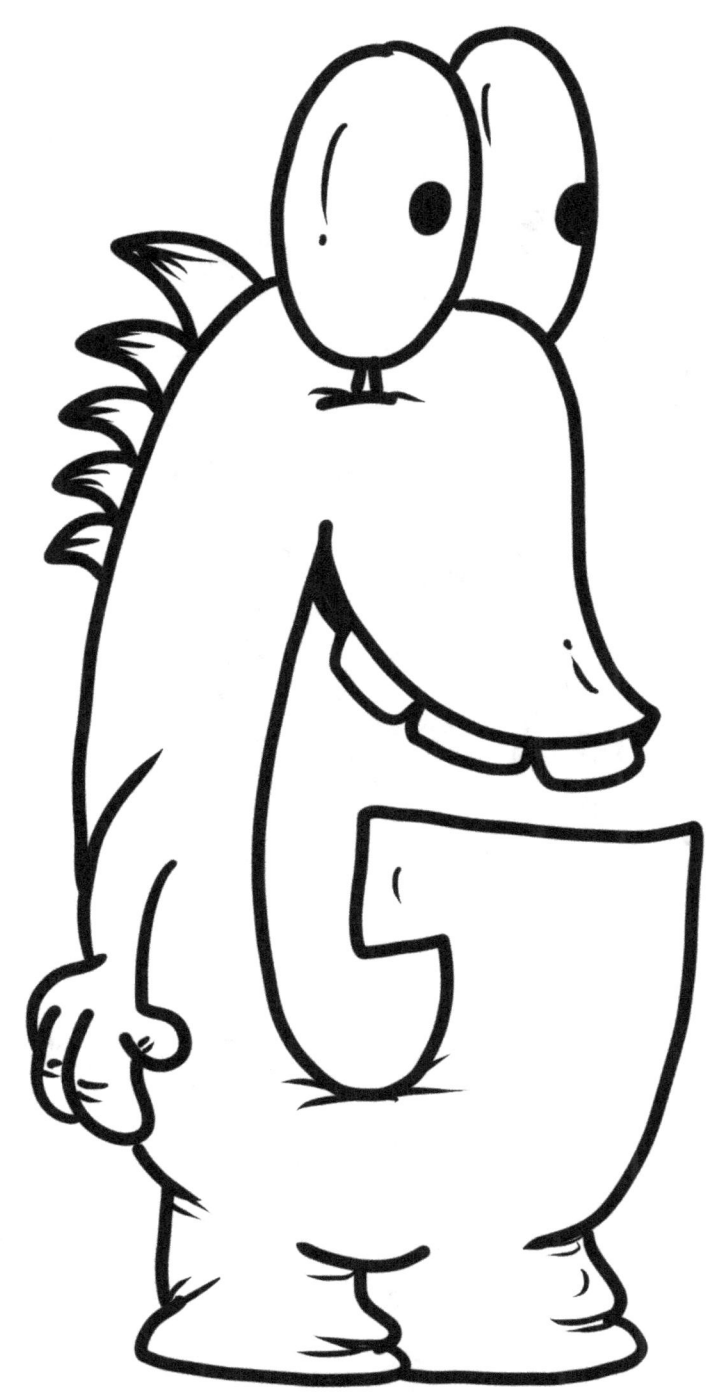

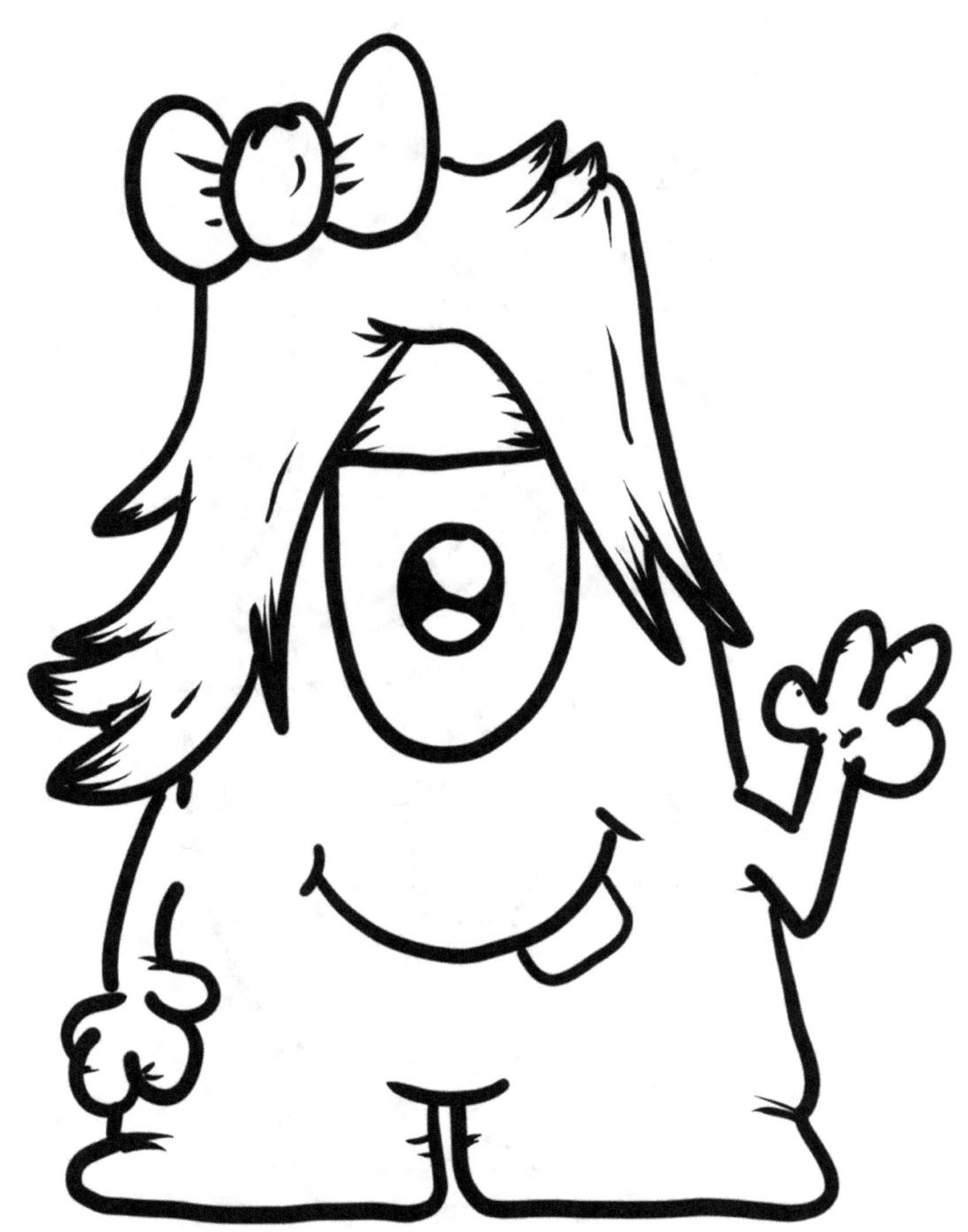

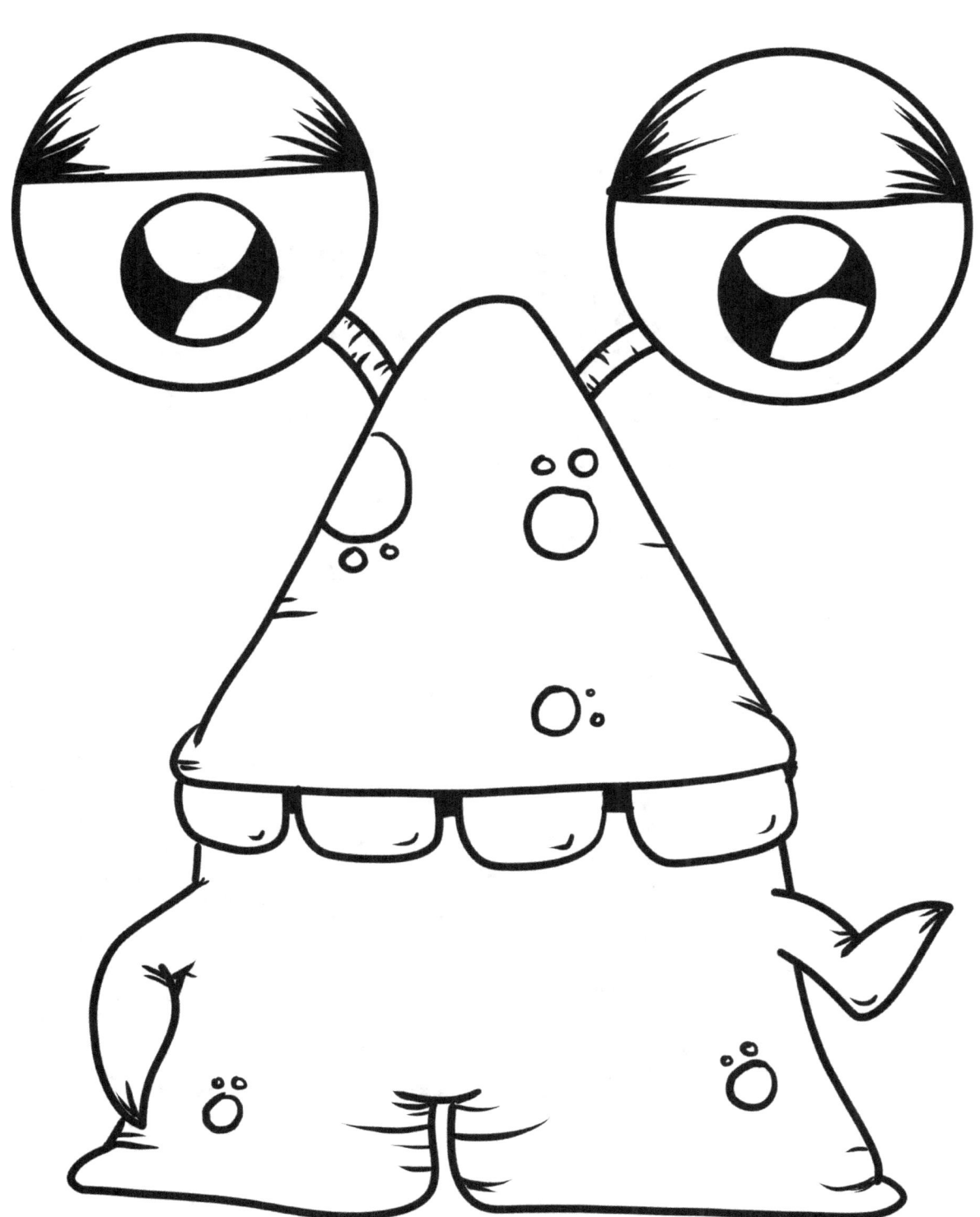

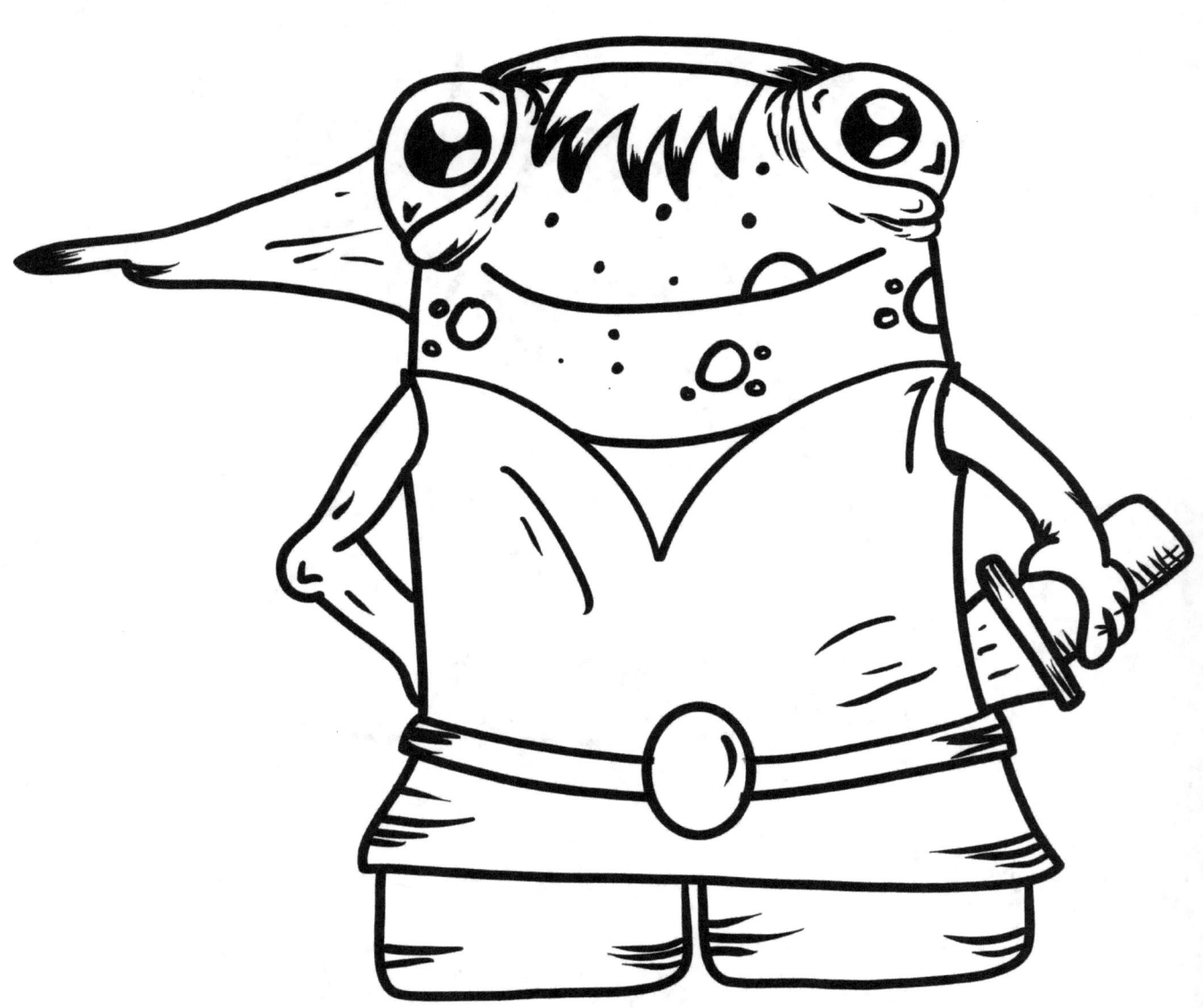

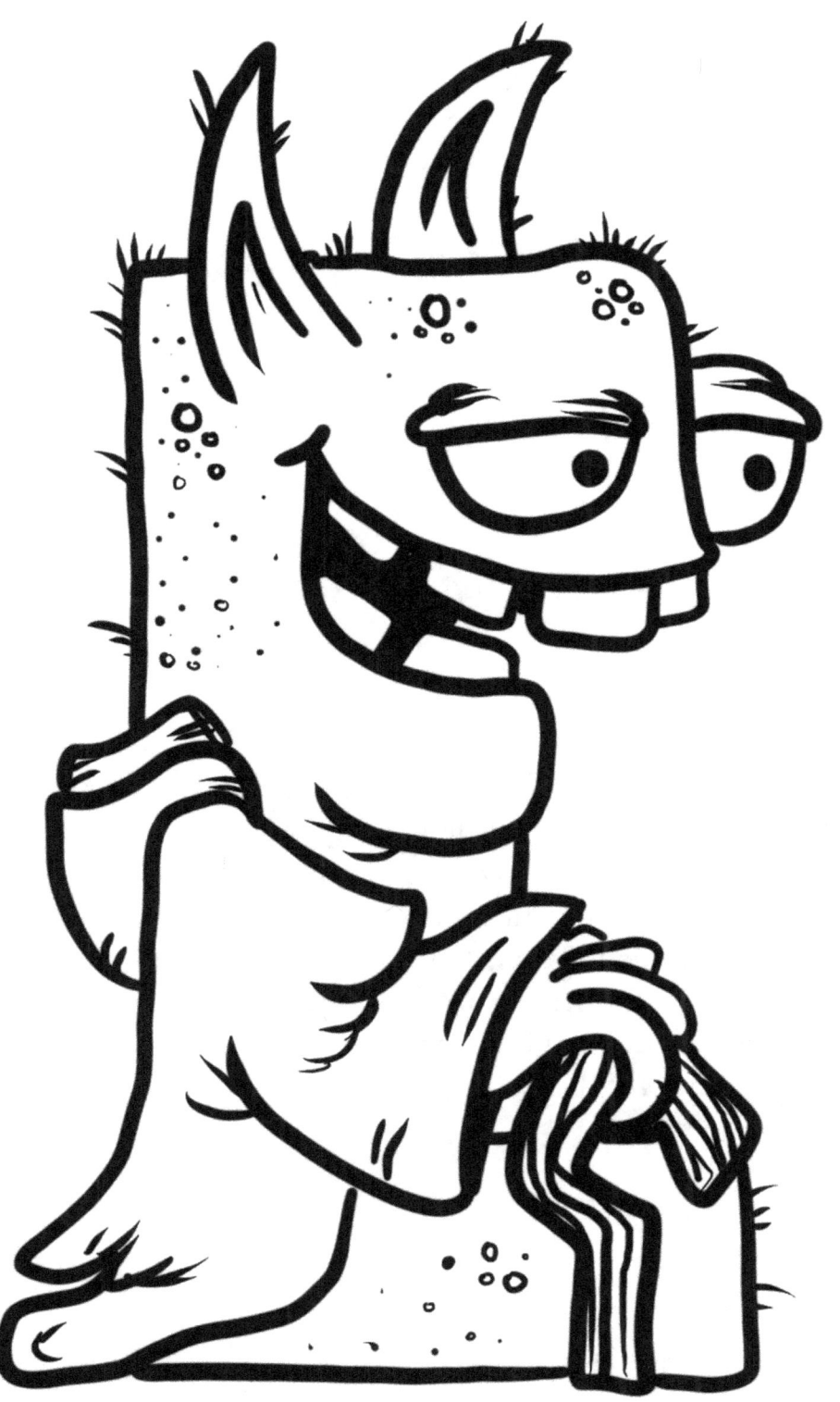

Special thanks to my family: Shaina, you always support all of my ideas, no matter how crazy they are. Landon, you are always my creative inspiration. Lila, you are my measure for whether an idea is good or not - if you like it, then it's good. Mom, thank you for pushing me to write and create these books. Without your everlasting support this book would not have happened. Dad, thanks for logic and laughter.

www.ingramcontent.com/pod-product-compliance
Lightning Source LLC
Chambersburg PA
CBHW062201220526
45470CB00009B/2892